DEMENTIA

A COMPREHENSIVE GUIDE TO UNDERSTANDING THE DISEASE

Rebecca Thomas Evans

D1713328

Contents

Dedication

This book is dedicated to My dad

I miss you so much!

Book Introduction

The memory lingers vividly in my mind, its sharpness undiminished by the passage of time. My father—the towering figure of my childhood, the man whose laughter filled our home, who steadied the back of my bicycle on countless summer evenings, who sat beside me, patient and kind, as I stumbled over the words of my first book—stood before me with a look of profound confusion. The bewilderment etched onto his face was a stark contrast to the image of the competent, sure-footed man I had always known. His eyes, once so keen and perceptive, now seemed clouded, as if a fog had rolled in and obscured the very memories that connected him to his surroundings, to his own identity, and heartbreakingly, to me, his daughter. We sat together, the hands of the clock marking the silent rhythm of our visit. I spoke of familiar stories, retold our shared memories in the hope that the sound of my voice might tether him back to me, even for a fleeting moment. For an instant—a brief, fragile moment—I saw a glimmer, a spark of recognition in his eyes, like the first ray of dawn piercing through the night. It flickered there, a weak but defiant signal that somewhere within the labyrinth of his fading mind, he knew me.

Then, it vanished, as ephemeral as a whisper carried away by the wind, and I was once again a stranger in his weary eyes. It was then that he posed the question, with a child-like curiosity that belied the gravity of the moment. "Who are you?" It was a question that seemed to hang heavily in the air between us, laden with the weight of all that was being lost to his illness.

I anchored myself to the simplicity of truth, as one does in moments too complex for elaborate words. "I'm Rebecca," I replied, the name feeling suddenly foreign on my tongue. His response was gentle, tinged with the faintest echoes of warmth and familiarity. "I know a Rebecca," he said with a smile that could light up the darkest of rooms. "She is a good egg." A smile found its way onto my face too, a reflection of his, as I absorbed the sweetness of that description. But within it, in that endearing phrase "good egg," lay the unbearable realization that he was clinging to scraps of a memory that no longer formed a complete picture.

That conversation became our last. The relentless march of time did not pause, and by the following morning, my father passed away. The grief hit me with the intensity of a sudden plunge into frigid waters on the coldest day of winter. It stunned me, left me gasping for breath and struggling to comprehend the reality that he was gone. In that moment, and in the endless moments that followed, I was enveloped by the cold clutch of loss, yet somewhere within, a warmth persisted — the lingering warmth of having been loved by a man who, for a time, had forgotten me, but who had once been my entire world.

Looking at what brought me here, let's face reality. If you take the time to read a newspaper, or if you switch on your TV or listen to the radio, it won't be long before you encounter the subject of dementia. There might be exciting news of a breakthrough in scientific research, or perhaps a story about a celebrity who has recently been diagnosed with the condition. It's also possible that you'll hear from an expert discussing a certain type of food we've all enjoyed in the past that is now being linked to an increased risk of developing dementia.

The frequent mentions of dementia in the media should not surprise us, as the occurrence of this condition is, unfortunately, becoming more common. The numbers are quite alarming. On average, every four seconds, somebody, somewhere around the world receives a life-changing diagnosis of dementia. With this constant ticking of the clock, the global tally of people living with dementia is rapidly increasing.

According to the World Health Organization, as we stand today, over thirty-five million people worldwide suffer from dementia. Each year, an additional 7.7 million new cases are identified, adding to this growing concern. Turning our attention closer to home, within the boundaries of the United States, an estimated 820,000 individuals are navigating the complexities of life with dementia. Alzheimer's Research United States has provided a sobering statistic—it is estimated that one out of every three persons within the United States will know someone very close to them, either a family member or a dear friend, who is battling with this disease.

These statistics aren't just numbers on paper or pixels on a screen; they represent a multitude of personal stories, families, and communities feeling the profound impact. Reflecting upon these figures brings to light the reality that dementia is not a distant concern—it's a present and growing issue that is touching the lives of millions.

With such a pervasive reach, it's clear why dementia has become a topic of frequent conversation and intense study. Researchers worldwide are tirelessly working towards finding a cure or effective treatments. In the meantime, awareness and understanding continue to grow, vital in supporting those affected by the condition.

Regrettably, the rising prevalence of dementia indicates that the necessity for medical advancements, support systems, and comprehensive care for those struggling is not just immediate but will be ongoing for many years to come. These sobering figures underscore the need for all of us to engage with this topic—whether it's through education, support, or advocacy—to confront a future where dementia becomes a challenge faced by fewer families rather than an inevitability for many.

About the Book

This book is meticulously crafted to offer a wide lens through which the reader can explore and understand not one, but four diseases that lead to dementia. It's comprehensive in nature, delving into the origin and progression of each disease, dissecting the complexities involved that ultimately culminate in the debilitating symptoms often witnessed in affected individuals.

A significant portion of this book is dedicated to describing the neuronal changes occurring within the brain as these diseases take hold, and the resulting cognitive decline. This unravelling of the changes gives readers a glimpse into the biological transformations synonymous with these conditions, fostering a better understanding of the symptoms they encounter, either personally or through loved ones. In an effort to bring clarity to the often perplexing world of dementia treatments, this book navigates through conventional medical interventions as well as holistic and complementary therapies. Readers are equipped with insights into what current science says about the effectiveness of various treatments, delivering guidance on what may or may not be beneficial in managing the symptoms or slowing disease progression.

Caregiving is a central theme, and therefore significant attention is given to equipping carers with practical strategies that will aid them in handling the more challenging aspects of the diseases as they advance. From managing difficult behaviors to providing dignified care, this book serves to lessen the burden and make the intricate caregiving process a little easier to manage. The contents go beyond medical advice by addressing essential topics such as planning for the future with will writing, which is particularly important to consider after a dementia diagnosis. It also delivers valuable insights on matters like selecting the most appropriate care facility, ensuring that readers have the necessary information to make informed decisions that align with their wants or those of their loved ones.

To enhance the learning experience, this book invites you to traverse on a 'choose your own path' adventure. While a traditional front-to-back read offers a sequence from diagnosis to end-of-life care, each chapter is intentionally written as a standalone entity, providing the flexibility to jump directly to topics that resonate or require immediate attention. Sprinkled throughout the chapters are sidebars — text boxes that can be described as the seasoning to the main dish. These are intended to provide additional context or fascinating trivia that enriches the reader's understanding of the topic at hand. Feel free to engage with these informative nuggets as you please. They are not critical for comprehension of the main text, so if they don't capture your interest, you can skip them without the worry of missing out on critical information.

The layout and structure of the book are purposefully designed to cater to varying preferences and needs. Whether you prefer a sequential learning process or random access to topics, the book is accommodating. The aim is to ensure that every reader, regardless of how they opt to engage with the content, comes away with a deeper knowledge of dementia and the confidence to face the challenges it poses. This resource is not just about presenting facts; it's about offering support, illumination, and understanding to those who find themselves navigating the murky waters of dementia, either directly or indirectly.

Chapter 1

Understanding the word "Dementia"

In this chapter,

> ➤ We'll explore:
> ➤ The fundamentals of dementia, beginning with a clear explanation of what dementia entails. We'll also examine the extent of this condition's impact on society, and how age plays a crucial role in its development.
> ➤ Additionally, we'll identify the primary four types of dementia, and consider other medical conditions that might lead to it.

Let's begin with a real life story…

Margaret, who once stood at the front of a classroom with unwavering confidence, was acclaimed for her razor-sharp wit and impressive memory – traits that not only distinguished her as an exemplary schoolteacher but also endeared her to countless students over the years. She had a remarkable gift for remembering details that many others would forget, such as every single student's name, even years after they'd left her classroom, and the exact dates of pivotal events in history.

However, as the years gracefully added to her life, Margaret began to encounter unsettling changes in her cognitive faculties. Little things at first, like misplacing her keys – an annoying occurrence that happens to everyone. But it was when she blanked on the name of a student she had always recalled fondly that Margaret sensed something might be wrong. These instances of lapses in memory weren't just rare mishaps anymore; they had begun to form a disturbing and relentless pattern of forgetfulness that couldn't be ignored.

This shift in her mental sharpness did not go unnoticed by her loved ones. Margaret's family, especially her devoted daughter Caroline, became increasingly concerned with her mother's growing absent-mindedness. In an act of both concern and love, Caroline accompanied Margaret to a neurological specialist, seeking clarity on these noticeable changes.

After thorough evaluations and tests, the neurologist confirmed what they had feared yet anticipated – Margaret was diagnosed with early-stage Alzheimer's disease. The news was undoubtedly difficult to process; the prospects that lay ahead were intimidating. Despite the fear and uncertainty swirling around the diagnosis, one thing remained steadfast for Margaret – the solid support system in her loving family. They rallied around her, determined to face the challenge as a united front.

Margaret's tale echoes the stories of millions across the globe who are confronted with the realities of Alzheimer's, a widespread and insidious variant of dementia. This condition silently weaves its way through the brain, progressively impeding the ability to remember, reason, and engage in basic daily activities.

The following passages intend to serve as a guide, a beacon of knowledge and understanding for those who might be treading the early stages of this path. By recognizing early signs such as difficulty recalling recent events or conversations, challenges in planning or problem solving, and misplacing things with increasing frequency, individuals and their families can seek medical advice promptly. This chapter is not only about the early recognition of Alzheimer's disease but also about forging ahead after the diagnosis—an endeavor that involves both practical strategies for coping with daily life and the exploration of treatments to slow the progression. It calls for a compassionate understanding of how Alzheimer's is indeed distinct from other dementias, emphasizing its unique symptomology and the trajectory it follows.

We can tackle Alzheimer's disease with more effectiveness, familiarity, and empathy by thoroughly comprehending these disparities. Margaret's journey, though fraught with challenges, is a testament to the power of awareness and the strength that comes from the support of loved ones. Together, with resources and a strong network of care, those affected by Alzheimer's can learn to adapt and find moments of joy amidst the trials.

If you're delving into the topic of dementia, comprehending its definition is paramount. Some view it as merely being prone to forgetfulness, misplacing glasses, or not remembering recent activities and names of loved ones. Others associate dementia with elderly individuals who appear disoriented, have mishaps with incontinence, and are noticeably irritable. However, these symptoms alone do not suffice for a dementia diagnosis.

The term 'dementia' entails a specific medical condition with a precise definition, ensuring the diagnosis is approached with the utmost seriousness. This chapter aims to demystify dementia, clarifying what it is and importantly, what it is not.

Let's talk about dementia like we're having a cup of coffee together. It's not one thing; it's a bunch of issues that mess with how the brain works.

The folks at the World Health Organization describe dementia as a scenario where someone's brain power dips more than you'd expect as they grow older. It's not just about those 'where did I put my keys?' moments – it's about struggling with thinking, figuring stuff out, remembering names, working with numbers, following a conversation, and making decisions. But hey, people with dementia are still awake and kicking, they're aware – it's just that sometimes things around them can feel mixed up.

To break it down further:

- When we say 'syndrome,' imagine it's like a collection of signals or clues that show up in someone with a certain health issue. Someone with dementia might be a whiz at remembering their shopping but might not remember whether they turned off the oven. It varies from person to person.
- 'Chronic' and 'progressive' sound serious, right? Well, 'chronic' just means it sticks around for a long time. And 'progressive' means it will probably get worse as time goes by. But keep in mind, for some people it's like a small leak in a faucet, and for others, it's more like a flood.
- When we talk about 'consciousness,' we mean that people with dementia are not out of it – they're awake and they know there's a world around them, even if it doesn't always make sense.

In plain speak, dementia comes from different brain diseases that lead to these tricky symptoms. Over time, they can get in the way of your thoughts, feelings, and daily doings; eventually, it can be tough to even tackle the everyday routine. But remember, dementia's a spectrum, where everyone's experience is a bit different – some people may face harder challenges than others. It's important to keep the conversation going, knowing that this is something many people and families deal with as they get older.

Understanding What Dementia Really Isn't

There's a lot of confusion out there about dementia, with countless myths floating around. To really understand dementia, it's just as crucial to know what it's not as it is to know what it is. I'm here to break down some common misunderstandings and set the record straight.

- **It's not a given that old age brings dementia.** Sure, getting older might increase the risk, but it's not just part and parcel of growing old. In reality, only about 1 in 14 people over 65 and 1 in 6 people over 80 are affected by dementia.
- **Thinking all dementia is Alzheimer's? Think again.** Alzheimer's is only one kind of brain condition that can cause dementia—there are actually several other types out there.
- **A slip-up in memory doesn't automatically mean dementia.** While those with dementia often struggle with remembering things, a diagnosis requires much more than just that. We're talking about a range of more complex symptoms, not just a momentary lapse in memory.
- **Not everyone with dementia will show aggression.** Some might get restless or snap, but this isn't the norm and it's often the result of how they're being treated or communicated with, not just the dementia doing its thing.

- **A diagnosis of dementia isn't the end of the road.** Yes, it's a chronic and progressively worsening condition, but there are all sorts of treatments and ways to cope that can help someone with dementia lead a meaningful life for many years.
- **Nursing homes aren't a foregone conclusion for everyone with dementia.** About one third of those with dementia might need that extra care in their later stages, but plenty of others get by just fine with support and love, right in their own homes.
- **Worried you'll definitely get dementia because your grandma has it? Breathe easy.** A few forms of dementia can be hereditary, but these are pretty rare. Just because it runs in the family doesn't mean you're destined to have it too. And in case you were worried, no, it's not contagious—you can't "catch" it from someone else.

So, there you go—I hope this helps clear up a few things about dementia. Remember, getting the full picture is key, and knowing what it's not is a big part of that.

Reflecting on the Dementia Diagnosis Data

Here's a startling fact to consider: every four seconds, somewhere in the world, someone gets the news that they're facing dementia. That's like 15 people getting this life-changing diagnosis every single minute. Picture watching your favorite soccer team on the field or settling into a cozy theater seat for the latest movie release; by the time you're done, 1,350 individuals have just heard those difficult words. When nighttime rolls around, you can count another 21,600 people facing the reality of dementia since the day began – that adds up to a staggering 7.7 million new cases each year.

Alzheimer's diagnosis involves several steps. Initially, doctors conduct physical examinations and check medical history to rule out other causes of memory loss such as stroke or tumor. They also perform cognitive tests to measure memory, language skills, problem-solving abilities and other thinking skills. Diagnostic tools have advanced tremendously over the years. Neuroimaging techniques such as MRI or PET scans provide detailed images of the brain which can help identify characteristic changes associated with Alzheimer's.

A study published in the Journal of Neurology and Neuroscience highlighted the importance of early diagnosis and intervention in slowing down the progression of Alzheimer's disease. This is because Alzheimer's disease is characterized by the buildup of plaques and tangles in the brain, which can be detected through specific diagnostic tests. Early diagnosis helps families prepare for what lies ahead and can lead to better management of symptoms through treatment plans tailored to each individual patient's needs. Cognitive testing forms a crucial part of diagnosing Alzheimer's disease. Tests assess various domains including memory recall, spatial ability, attention span and language use. These tasks gauge whether there are significant cognitive deficits that interfere with daily living activities. The Mini-Mental State Examination (MMSE) is one such test widely used across health facilities globally for screening cognitive impairment in elderly patients.

According to studies, the Mini-Mental State Examination (MMSE) is one of the most commonly used cognitive tests for Alzheimer's. It assesses different areas of cognition including memory, attention, language, and spatial skills. However, it's important to note that while MMSE is useful in identifying cognitive impairment, it cannot conclusively diagnose Alzheimer's on its own. Another test often used is the Montreal Cognitive Assessment (MoCA), which is considered more sensitive than MMSE in detecting mild cognitive impairment - a stage often preceding Alzheimer's. Emotional evaluations also play a significant role in diagnosing Alzheimer's disease. Depression and anxiety are common in people with Alzheimer's, so evaluating a person's mood can provide valuable insights into their condition. Interestingly enough, one distinguishing feature of Alzheimer's compared to other forms of dementia is the pattern of memory loss. While short-term memory loss is common in all types of dementia, research suggests that those with Alzheimer's tend to lose their episodic memory - remembering specific events - earlier than those with other forms of dementia.

Biomarkers are biological substances that change in response to a disease. In Alzheimer's, scientists have identified specific biomarkers in cerebrospinal fluid and blood that can indicate the presence of the disease even before symptoms appear. The progression towards biomarker-based diagnosis represents an exciting frontier in Alzheimer's research. Greater accuracy and early detection can lead to improved treatment outcomes and may potentially pave the way towards prevention strategies. A study published in The Lancet Neurology highlights that "blood biomarkers could revolutionize Alzheimer's disease diagnosis by enabling early detection and intervention."

Alzheimer's disease is a challenging journey not just for those diagnosed but also for their loved ones. But understanding the diagnostic process is crucial as it paves the way for better management of this condition. Early detection allows families to plan ahead, initiate suitable treatments and confirm their loved one leads a life with dignity and care despite dementia. By recognizing these diagnostic steps, you will be equipped to navigate through this complex terrain ensuring your loved one gets the best possible care.

Therefore, if you or your loved ones are experiencing signs associated with Alzheimer's such as memory loss that disrupts daily life or challenges in planning or solving problems; seek medical advice immediately. Early detection means early intervention - which could significantly improve quality-of-life outcomes for people living with this condition and may help slow down the progression of this devastating illness! Remember that while there isn't now a cure for Alzheimer's disease; science continues to advance at an unprecedented pace – every new discovery brings us one step closer towards finding effective treatments. After removing cases from our conversation that aren't really dementia, we can get down to the nitty-gritty of who is actually dealing with this diagnosis. And I have to say, the picture isn't very cheerful.

It's estimated that about half, or even more, of the people living with dementia haven't been diagnosed yet. When you think about those numbers, the situation seems pretty grim.

Without overdramatizing, we need to be clear-eyed about the challenge we're all facing. This awareness is key – not just so policymakers and health experts can figure out what kind of support and care will be needed as dementia becomes increasingly common, but also so that folks who are grappling with the condition, along with their families, know they're not in this alone.

The facts, according to Alzheimer's Disease International, lay it out plainly:

- Right now, around 44.4 million people globally are living with dementia.

- They expect that number to double by 2030, and triple by 2050.
- Most of the people with dementia (62%) live in developing countries, which is likely to increase to 71% by 2050.
- When you look at the financial side, we're talking about $600 billion dollars spent worldwide on dementia care.

To put that into perspective:

- If dementia were its own nation, it would be the 18th largest economy, sitting right between Turkey and Indonesia in terms of size.
- If dementia were a company, it would be the biggest in the world, out-earning giants like Walmart and Exxon Mobil.

There are going to be major differences in how this increase in dementia diagnoses throws weight around across the globe. Estimates suggest a 90% increase in Europe, more than 200% in Asia and the Americas, and a mind-blowing 345% in Africa. Even more concerning is that out of 193 countries in the World Health Organization, only 13 have a national plan to deal with dementia, and none of them are in Africa.

In the United States, the numbers provided by Alzheimer's Research United States and the Alzheimer's Society paint a clear picture of where the country stands in the bigger global context:

- We've got 820,000 folks living with dementia today, which translates to 25 million people who personally know someone battling it.
- That number will likely double by 2050.

- Women make up two-thirds of the dementia cases in the United States.
- The economic toll is heavy—dementia costs more than cancer and heart disease combined, totaling $23 billion per year.

Despite all the resources funneled into managing dementia, the investment in research is considerably lower compared to cancer, with dementia research receiving around $50 million annually versus the $590 million poured into cancer studies.

Writing this all down really brings home the severity and scale of what we're up against with dementia. It underscores the importance of ramping up our efforts and support to tackle this challenge head-on.

The Connection Between Getting Older and Dementia

It's pretty much common knowledge that the older you get, the more likely it is you might face dementia. To give you an idea, if you're younger than 65, the chances are pretty low — less than 2% actually. But as the years roll by, the risk goes up. Here's a quick breakdown from the Alzheimer's Society:

- If you're between 40 and 64, the chances are like 1 in 1,400.
- From 65 to 69, it jumps to 1 in 100.
- In your 70s, the odds are 1 in 25.
- And once you hit the 80s and beyond, it's about 1 in 6.

Now, we're all living longer thanks to better healthcare, science, and all that techy stuff. Humans didn't always have it this good. Once upon a time — think 30,000 years back — most folks didn't celebrate many birthdays, like under 30. Even in the 1800s, making it to 40 was a big deal. But now, things are different. The average chap in the United States can expect to kick around for nearly 79 years, and women can top off at an impressive 82.7.

Keep in mind, this is an average. In the United States, your mileage may vary with factors like wealth and where you live. And it's a sad reality that in some places, like Chad, folks have a shorter ride, averaging at just 49.5 years.

But times are a-changing', and we're looking at more and more people celebrating their 65th birthdays and beyond. Right now, there are 10 million people over 65 in the United States. By 2035, we're expecting about 5.5 million more! And by the middle of the century? A whopping 19 million.

Crazy to think, but a kid born in the United States in 2030 could easily blow out 91 candles on his birthday cake, or maybe even 95 if he's a she. But here's the catch: as our number of birthdays increase, so does the likelihood of dementia creeping up on us. That means we're probably going to see a lot more of it in the future because of all those extra years we're racking up.

In a nutshell, as life expectancy goes up, we might have to get even smarter about tackling dementia. It's a challenge, sure — but considering how far we've come, it's one we could be ready to take on.

Understanding Dementia Beyond Alzheimer's

It's a common mistake to think that dementia and Alzheimer's are the same thing. While Alzheimer's is a big part of dementia, there are many other reasons why someone might have dementia.

We should also talk about something called mild cognitive impairment. It's not quite dementia, but it's not a normal part of getting older, either. For about 40% of folks with this mild memory trouble, dementia is unfortunately what's next. However, the other 60% won't see their condition worsen. Sometimes, if the cause is something like depression or an infection, they might even get better.

When talk turns to dementia, it's kind of like hearing about the 'big five' animals on an African safari. You've got the top stars - lions, elephants, buffalos, leopards, and rhinos. Dementia has its own heavy hitters, the 'big four': Alzheimer's, vascular dementia, Lewy body disease, and fronto-temporal dementia. Here's a down-to-earth run-down on them.

Alzheimer's Disease

Alzheimer's is the big kahuna -- the most common type of dementia around the globe. In the United States, for instance, it accounts for 62% of all dementia cases. That's over 400,000 folks dealing with this illness. What happens is that this disease causes nasty protein build-ups in brain cells, which basically makes them shut down. Symptoms start affecting memory, mood, and the ability to do daily tasks, and as the disease spreads, things get worse.

Vascular Dementia

Next in line is vascular dementia. This one is linked to about 17% of dementia cases in the United States. It hits because the blood vessels in the brain get damaged, messing with blood flow and oxygen getting to the brain cells. The symptoms can look a lot like Alzheimer's, but they depend on what part of the brain is getting less blood. Some people might also experience stroke-like symptoms, where they can't move parts of their body or talk properly. And there's this thing called mixed dementia, which affects about 10% of patients. That's when someone has a combo of Alzheimer's and vascular dementia.

Lewy Body Disease

Then we have Lewy body disease, the rarer kind you don't 'see' often, affecting around 4% of those with dementia. These Lewy bodies are actually protein deposits hurting brain cells, kind of like Alzheimer's, but it's also linked with Parkinson's disease. People with this type of dementia might have muscle issues, see things that aren't there, and have trouble moving around.

Fronto-Temporal Dementia

The least common of the 'big four' is fronto-temporal dementia, which is found in about 2% of dementia cases in the United States. It's especially noteworthy because it's the type most likely to show up in folks under 65. Targeting the frontal and temporal lobes of the brain, this one messes with memory and personality. Symptoms can include weird or inappropriate behavior, not caring about personal hygiene, repetitive speech, a hankering for sweets, and just a general lack of drive. That's the nutshell version of dementia's 'big four'. Each one is unique, with its own set of challenges, but knowledge is power. Understand what's out there, and you're better equipped to face it.

Understanding Mild Cognitive Impairment — Is It Early Dementia?

Have you noticed that as folks get older, their sharp wit might not cut as quickly as it used to, or that they often forget where they left the keys? It's normal to see a few hiccups in memory and brain function with age. But there's something called mild cognitive impairment (MCI) that's a bit like having a weaker version of dementia — imagine "dementia lite."

First off, dementia is a tough cookie — it messes with memory and also jumbles up other thinking skills. Plus, it can really throw off a person's mood and ability to do everyday stuff. Now, MCI sits in the middle; it's not a normal part of aging, but it's not as severe as full-blown dementia either. When someone has MCI, they may notice that their thinking skills aren't what they used to be, but they can still do their daily routine and feel okay emotionally.

Interestingly, not everyone with MCI will get worse. In fact, about 60% of folks with MCI stay the same or even get better. But, for others, especially those with Alzheimer's, MCI might hint that dementia may follow.

The Lowdown on Aging Brains

Everyone knows that getting older comes with its own set of quirks. Our bodies creak a bit more, and our memories might fuzz around the edges. But contrary to what we used to think, older brains don't just lose a bunch of cells and call it a day. Most people end their lives with nearly as many brain cells as they started with.

Our brains do shrink a bit — about 10% over our adult life — but that's not the whole story behind forgetting names or losing track of conversations. The 'senior moments' come from a mix of things like weaker connections between neurons (the brain's messengers), bumps in brain inflammation, a dip in blood supply, and the wear and tear from facing off with environmental free radicals, like oxygen and nitrogen.

When you put all that together, plus the brain shrinkage, you get the typical age-related changes we see. Reactions are slower, and puzzles might take longer than before. It's pretty standard to notice these shifts, although some lucky people zip through their 90s without missing a beat.

When the Brain Ages Differently

Now, with MCI, the game's changed. The symptoms are a bit more intense than just your usual age-related stuff. People might realize they:

- Forget things more often
- Have trouble keeping up with discussions
- Can't make decisions as easily
- Get lost more often
- Start to wobble on concentration and focus

MCI's seriousness and whether it leans toward actual dementia can be measured using something called the Global Deterioration Scale (GDS) that Dr. Barry Reisberg cooked up back in '82. It has seven stages — from "all good" to "whoops, early dementia is here."

- **Stage 1:** Neither the doctor nor the person spots any problems.
- **Stage 2:** Only the person sees the problem, maybe with remembering people's names, but test scores are still all right.
- **Stage 3:** MCI kicks in. Jobs and social life get a little rocky, and tests might show a few blips.

- **Stage 4:** Memory and task management get tricky, like handling money or traveling. Sometimes, people might not want to admit it, signaling the early stages of dementia.
- **Stage 5:** At this point, a person can still handle their daily routines, like getting dressed, eating, and using the bathroom. They may need a small reminder now and then, especially since they might start forgetting the names of people and places.
- **Stage 6:** Things get harder in this stage. The person might not remember recent events at all and needs much more help with daily activities, possibly even moving into a care home. They might struggle with continence too.
- **Stage 7:** This is a tough stage where the person has severe dementia. They rely entirely on others for care and can barely move or talk.

What Causes Mild Cognitive Impairment and How to Prevent It

Mild cognitive impairment can be an early sign of dementia, often due to similar brain changes seen in Alzheimer's disease. This includes protein build-up, reduced blood flow to the brain, and shrinkage of the memory-related hippocampus.

While there's no magic cure for this stage, you can do a lot to keep your blood flowing and your mind sharp! Control your blood pressure, eat healthy, quit tobacco, drink responsibly, and stay active.

And did you know? Keeping your mind active is great too! Solve puzzles, read regularly, and enjoy hobbies that make you think. These activities are not just fun; they may also help your brain.

Are Expensive Brain Games Worth It?

You've seen those fancy brain games that promise to sharpen your mind and keep dementia at bay. But hold on to your wallet—research by the Alzheimer's Society and BBC's "Bang Goes the Theory" found that they might not be the miracle cure we hope for.

A big study called 'Brain Test Britain' showed that while people got good at the games themselves, those skills didn't really improve their memory or planning abilities in everyday life. The takeaway? You might be just as well off with regular puzzles and crosswords that don't cost a penny. Remember, staying mentally fit is a bit like keeping physically fit. It's less about expensive gadgets and more about consistency and enjoying the activities you do. Keep those brain muscles flexing, but be kind to yourself and know that the best tools for your mind might already be at your fingertips.

Sometimes people experience symptoms that seem like dementia, but these symptoms can actually come from a bunch of other medical issues. Thankfully, these conditions are not the same as dementia—they don't keep getting worse over time and can often be fixed.

Imagine feeling confused or struggling with daily tasks—these can be signs of dementia, but they can also come from something else entirely. That's why when folks talk to their doctor about this kind of stuff, doctors usually run some simple blood and urine tests first. They do this to check if there's something else going on in the body that might be causing these symptoms. There are quite a few things that could mess with your brain functions or hormones and give you a tough time with clear thinking or memory. And sometimes, if you're really sick with something else, like an infection, it can make you feel all mixed up too. Plus, we all know drinking too much alcohol over a long time can make it hard to think straight or remember things.

It's pretty important to figure out what's really going on, because if it's one of these other conditions—and not dementia—there's a good chance it can be treated and you'll start to feel like yourself again.

Some brain and nerve conditions can show signs that look a bit like dementia but have their own special symptoms too. Doctors usually check to make sure these other illnesses aren't playing a part before they settle on dementia as the diagnosis:

- **Parkinson's disease**: It's not just a movement disorder; folks with Parkinson's are actually more likely to also get dementia. About 2% of all dementia cases come from Parkinson's disease. They share quite a bit with Lewy body disease, so people might have trouble thinking, moving smoothly, and could see things that aren't there (hallucinations), feel pretty moody, or get easily upset. Unfortunately, some medicines that help with Parkinson's movement troubles, like shaking and muscle stiffness, can make dementia signs worse.
- **Multiple sclerosis (MS)**: Here, the protective coating on your nerve cells called myelin gets damaged. That messes with how nerves send messages. When the injured nerves are in the brain's cortex—which is the big boss for all our high-level thinking tasks—people can find themselves forgetting stuff or having a hard time solving problems.

- **Normal pressure hydrocephalus**: This one involves too much cerebrospinal fluid building up around the brain and spinal cord where it normally cushions and delivers nutrients. In excess, this fluid starts hurting nerve cells. People around 55 to 60 years old might start to see dementia-like symptoms, have a tough time walking, or can't control their bladder. Draining the fluid can really help, and if it's done early, there's a good 80% chance of nipping the symptoms in the bud.
- **Creutzfeldt–Jakob disease (CJD)**: Luckily, this scary brain disease is rare. You might know the variant type from the whole mad cow disease panic. CJD can spread through these infectious proteins called prions that quickly chew up brain tissue and lead to death, usually within a year. Heartbreakingly, it brings on dementia, makes people unsteady on their feet, causes speech to slur, interferes with bladder control, and can lead to blindness.
- **Huntington's disease**: This one is a real doozy and is passed down through families. One wrong move on chromosome 4, and if one parent has it, each kid has a 50% chance of getting it too. Sadly, symptoms don't show up until middle age, but when they begin, they don't stop—dementia sets in, and folks have irregular, jerky movements and go through big mood and personality shifts.

Understanding these conditions helps us see why doctors need to be super thorough before calling it dementia. And knowing about them can also spark compassion and support for those affected by these tough diseases.

Understanding Hormonal and Nutritional Impacts on Memory

Sometimes, memory problems or confusion can be tied back to hormonal imbalances or nutritional issues. The good news? Unlike some of the more serious brain-related conditions, these can often be turned around with the right treatment.

- **Struggles with Cortisol – Addison's and Cushing's Disease**: Think of cortisol as your body's built-in alarm system. It's pretty important. But sometimes, things go haywire. In Addison's disease, your body doesn't make enough cortisol, while Cushing's disease means you've got too much. Either way, it messes with your body's minerals like sodium and potassium, and the next thing you know, you're feeling all sorts of confused. But here's the comforting part: once doctors treat the underlying issue, you can start feeling like yourself again.
- **When Sugar Levels Swing – Diabetes**: Ever felt all muddled when your stomach's growling, or after you've had way too much cake? That's because blood sugar levels can really mess with your head. Doctors often see folks who are super confused because their sugar levels are either in the basement or through the roof. Sort those levels out, and voilà – clarity returns.
- **The Thyroid's Influence**: The thyroid is this neat little gland in your neck, and it makes a hormone called thyroxine that pretty much sets the pace for your body. Too much thyroxine, and it's like you're on fast-forward; too little, and everything slows to a crawl. Both of these extremes can leave you befuddled. But straightening out your thyroid levels can clear up the confusion.
- **Overactive Parathyroids – Hyperparathyroidism**: Behind your thyroid are

these teeny glands called parathyroids, and they help balance calcium and other substances in your blood. If they start going overboard, the calcium levels spike, and that can lead to personality changes, confusion, or even coma if it gets too severe. Thankfully, treating this brings things back to normal.

- **The Mystery of Missing B12**: Vitamin B12 is super important - it's in stuff like fish, chicken, eggs, and milk. Your body needs a helper protein to absorb it, but sometimes, a hitch happens – not enough of it is made, or something destroys it, and you end up not getting enough B12. This vitamin is crucial for nerve health – think of it as the body's electrical wiring insulation. Low B12 can make your hands and feet feel weird, mess with your mood, and fog up your memory. But the fix is relatively straightforward – B12 injections bypass the stomach obstacles and can help reverse these issues.

When it comes to your memory and overall well-being, these hormonal and nutritional sideshows can have quite the impact, but being in the know and getting the right care can make all the difference. It's all about bringing things back into balance so you can feel good and clear-headed again.

Drinking too much alcohol can be dangerous, and it's not just because it's addictive. When you drink more than you should, it can really harm your body, especially your liver and brain, in ways that might make you think of someone with dementia.

Take cirrhosis for example. Drinking a lot of alcohol can hurt your liver cells so much that they can't do their job properly. And it's not just alcohol – bad luck like getting a virus like hepatitis or your own body turning against you (that's the autoimmune stuff) can mess up your liver, too. When the liver is shot, toxic substances start building up in your blood. These poisons can kill brain cells and lead to a bunch of problems like confusion, forgetting stuff, personality changes, and acting out of character. Sometimes, doctors can treat these brain issues if they fix up the liver damage, but it's serious business and can even be deadly.

Then there's something called Korsakoff's syndrome, named after the smart doctor who figured it out. You see it a lot in heavy drinkers, where downing too much alcohol keeps your body from taking in thiamine, which is a super-important B vitamin. You need thiamine to keep your nerve cells happy, and not having enough can make you forgetful and change the way you act. But here's some good news – if you stop drinking and start taking thiamine supplements, it can really help fix things.

The bottom line is, alcohol is no joke when it comes to your health. If you or someone you know is struggling with drinking, it's never too late to ask for help and start turning things around.

Having an infection

This can really mess with your head, particularly if you're older. You might start feeling confused or out of sorts, and it's not just you—it's actually pretty common. This confusion can happen when nasty bugs like viruses or bacteria attack the brain, produce harmful toxins in our blood, or just generally wear the body down through things like fevers or not drinking enough water.

When we talk about this sudden confusion, we sometimes use a fancy word from the past, "delirium." A few usual suspects that can cause this kind of trouble include:

- **Urinary Tract Infections:** Think of annoying conditions like cystitis where your bladder gets inflamed, or pyelonephritis which is a serious kidney infection.
- **Chest Infections:** These can range from a rough bout of bronchitis all the way up to heavy-duty pneumonia.
- **Severe Viral Infections:** The flu can knock you down hard and muddle your thinking.
- **Brain Infections:** Meningitis and encephalitis are big words for infections that either inflame the protective layers around the brain and spinal cord or go directly after the brain cells themselves.

It's important to catch these infections early because they can throw a real wrench in the works, especially for the brain. Always keep an eye out for these signs, and take it seriously if you or a loved one start feeling unexpectedly confused—it could be more than just an off day.

Even with the best intensions, medicine doesn't always do what we'd hope. While doctors stick to the principle of 'first, do no harm', and medications are supposed to make us feel better, things can go sideways. Every one of us reacts differently to treatment, and in a perfect situation, every therapy would be tailor-made just for us.

Unfortunately, the world's not perfect, and sometimes, despite careful prescribing, the medicines we take can make us feel worse instead of better. This is particularly true for seniors. Here are a few common meds that can sometimes lead to confusion:

- Anxiety meds like diazepam (you might know it as Valium)
- Heavy-duty painkillers, including tramadol, codeine, and morphine
- Steroids such as prednisolone, which are often used for long-term issues like bronchitis and arthritis
- Seizure medications like carbamazepine and phenytoin
- Anticholinergics, which cover certain allergy pills and drugs for conditions like overactive bladder, like oxybutynin

Remember, each person's experience with medication can be very different, so it's important to stay observant and talk to a doctor if something doesn't feel right.

Chapter 2

Spotting the Symptoms

In This Chapter, We will be:

- Recognizing early signs of dementia
- Knowing when there's a problem with memory or thinking

- Understanding emotional changes
- Noticing when daily activities become challenging

When we're sick, it helps a lot when doctors figure out exactly what's wrong – like telling a bad cold from the flu. Identifying the problem is key to getting the right help and knowing what to expect.

This chapter dives into what symptoms pop up when someone might have dementia. I share insights that help doctors pinpoint which type of dementia a person might be dealing with. It's all about offering a guiding hand as you or a loved one navigates this condition.

Spotting the Early Signs of Dementia

It's true that each person may face dementia in slightly different ways. However, there are a few signs that can give us a heads-up that it might be beginning to show up. In these initial phases, it's key not to worry too much or think that every time we forget something or feel mixed up, it's because of dementia. After all, our memories often change as we get older, and that's totally normal. It's also crucial to remember that dementia is a lot more than just a bit of forgetfulness.

We've all had those days when our heads are not quite in the game. Whether we're tired, a bit down, or simply lost in something really interesting, it happens to the best of us. Missing an appointment or overcooking dinner because we're caught up in a great chat? Yep, been there.

But when these little slip-ups start happening all the time, it might be time to take a closer look. It's normal for anyone to forget things now and then, but if it's happening so much that living an everyday life starts to feel tricky, that could be a sign of a bigger issue. If you or a loved one is struggling not just with memory, but also finding the right words or getting confused over day-to day tasks like handling money or making a well-known dish, it might be more than just 'senior moments.' This could be true especially if there's a shift in how they feel about joining in on social activities, or if they seem more down or unsure of themselves than usual.

It's important to remember that dementia isn't only about forgetting things. It can touch on different parts of a person's daily life. If you're noticing these changes, it could be time to reach out to a doctor for a chat. Remember, it's not just about what's forgotten, but about supporting each other through what's remembered and found anew.

Top Early Signs of Dementia to Watch For

It's hard to always know what to look out for when it comes to dementia, but I've put together a list that just about every expert agrees on.

1. Frequent Memory Lapses

We all forget things, that's normal as we age. But we usually remember them later, right? With dementia, that doesn't happen—what's forgotten stays forgotten, which is problematic because it involves stuff we need daily like:

- Important dates or events
- Our usual driving routes
- Where we placed important papers
- The names and faces of people we know

2. Struggling to Plan or Fix Problems

Take a grandma, for instance. She could whip up a Sunday feast without breaking a sweat. But when dementia started to set in, she just couldn't get the timings right anymore. She ended up with burnt veggies and undercooked meat more often than not, leaving grandpa to step in as head chef to avoid an empty table.

Signs also include getting muddled with:

- Using bank cards
- Understanding bank statements
- Filling up the car with gas

3. Trouble Finding the Right Words

We've all been there, searching for that one word mid-conversation or during a talk, and when it finally hits you, the relief is immense. But for someone with early dementia, words can slip away often. This can make talking so frustrating. They might even use a similar but incorrect word, like saying "kick ball" instead of "football," or "hand clock" for a watch.

Following conversations or socializing can also become daunting, especially with background noise, as it gets tougher to keep up.

4. Time and Place Confusion

Imagine forgetting the date, time, or even where you are and how you got there.

5. Decreased Judgement

People dealing with early dementia may notice a dip in their decision-making skills. Someone who's usually careful with money might start buying unnecessary stuff, or dress inappropriately for the weather—like bundling up for the beach or wearing nearly nothing in the rain.

Remember, these signs can be subtle at first. It's all about staying observant and supportive for our loved ones as they may not notice these changes themselves. If you spot these signs, reaching out to a professional for guidance is the next best step.

6. Clumsiness and Spatial Issues

Maybe you've noticed someone you care about is seeming a bit clumsier than usual or having trouble with things like parking the car. They might bump into furniture more often or have a few more close calls than before. This might be because they're finding it harder to judge distances or how big things are - a challenge sometimes linked to the early stages of dementia.

7. Misplacing Items

We all misplace our keys or phone occasionally, and usually, we can backtrack our steps to find them. But if someone starts losing the ability to do this, often leaving things in unusual spots (think slippers in the kitchen fridge!), it could be a sign of dementia. Everyday items might start to disappear, which can be pretty distressing.

8. Mood Swings

We all know teenagers can be a whirlwind of emotions - one minute you're the worst parent, the next, you're the hero. While those highs and lows tend to level out as we become adults, they can reappear in the early stages of dementia. Sudden shifts to sadness or anger or even depression can happen, and it can be hard to tell if it's the dementia causing these emotions or the other way around.

9. Loss of Motivation

We all have days when we're just not feeling it, whether it's work, hobbies, or hanging out with friends. But it's usually a temporary feeling. For someone facing dementia, the drive to engage in their normal activities might fade away. They might need a gentle nudge to remind them or encourage them to join in with the group.

10. Personality Shifts

When dementia is on the horizon, personality changes can be a real giveaway. But not everyone will change in the same way - a shy person might become unexpectedly outgoing, while someone who's usually the heart of the party might start keeping to themselves. You might notice they become confused, suspicious, withdrawn, or show a side of themselves that just isn't like them.

These examples show that dementia is so much more than just a bit of forgetfulness. To identify it correctly, at least two of these signs will usually be present, sometimes starting off subtle. Over time, though, these signs become part of someone's everyday life, making it clearer that dementia is developing.

In the next part, we'll take a closer look at these symptoms, which can deepen with time. They can affect the way a person thinks, their emotions, and day-to-day abilities. Remember, these symptoms overlap a lot and vary greatly from person to person. Also, different types of dementia can have their own unique signs - like those found in Alzheimer's or Lewy body dementia. It's also worth noting that some people might experience very few of these signs, so what we go over is just a general guide and not a prediction of what every person with dementia will go through.

Understanding Memory Loss in Dementia

When someone has dementia, they often face tough challenges with their memory and thinking abilities. Imagine a world where your memories start to blur, decisions become hard, and even familiar streets seem like uncharted territory.

The Fog of Forgetting

But these aren't unique tales. Dementia can twist the concept of time, preserving distant memories while yesterday's lunch fades into oblivion. It's as if the brain holds onto the far past—the wars lived through, the childhood memories—yet lets the present slip away like sand through fingers.

Short-term vs. Long-term Memory

Imagine trying to tackle your daily tasks but you can't recall your to-do list, whom you're meeting, or where your keys are. This is the reality for those with dementia. They might live with a treasure trove of long-gone moments, yet struggle to remember what they did just moments ago.

Remembering Faces and Places

Names, faces, and places—those can get jumbled up in dementia too. Even in a room full of loved ones, a person may feel lost among strangers. It's even harder when it affects their work life, unable to recognize their boss or colleagues. And when it comes to navigating spaces, even a trip to the local shop can turn into a maze, with every turn and street sign looking alien and confounding.

The Sense of Self

If you've noticed individuals with dementia stay close to their caregivers or ask the same questions repeatedly, it's not just for conversation. This behavior often comes from a place of seeking comfort and grounding, as they try to hold onto their sense of who they are now. It's pretty common for folks with memory troubles to lose their way, even on roads they've traveled a hundred times before. People who have dementia might also roam around a lot, which ups the chances they might end up someplace unfamiliar.

This sort of wandering isn't just walking around without reason – it's actually more like they're walking with a goal in mind. It's not always clear for those taking care of them why they might decide to roam, but there are a few guesses:

- **Old Habits:** For someone who always loved a good stroll, or who walked everywhere they went, it's natural to want to keep that up.
- **Curbing Boredom:** Being stuck with nothing to do can get pretty dull, especially when someone withdraws from work and socializing as their condition gets more serious. A walk can be a nice change of scenery and give a sense of purpose.
- **Extra Energy:** If they were usually buzzing around and staying active, being cooped up might make them restless. A simple walk can be an easy fix.
- **A Touch of Confusion:** Sometimes, a person with dementia sets off with a task in mind but ends up getting mixed up along the way. They might look

for things that feel familiar to help them get their bearings. Other times, they can get the time of day wrong, and before you know it, they're outside thinking it's daytime when it's still night. In more serious cases, they may go looking for people from their past.

- **Easing Discomfort:** If someone's living with arthritis, sitting still for too long can really make their joints hurt. Walking can help loosen up those joints and ease discomfort for a while.
- **Finding Something or Someone:** They might be on a mission to find a special place, maybe an old home or the house they grew up in. Or they might be trying to find friends, family, or even parents who passed away a long time ago.

Understanding why someone with dementia might wander can help us respond with kindness and help keep them safe. Remember, every step for them means something – even if we don't always get it right away.

Dealing with Emotional Changes

When someone has dementia, their emotions can get really tangled up, and "emotional roller-coaster" isn't just a saying. It's a real thing that can happen. This can make things really tough for families and caregivers who have to deal with the ups and downs.

Handling Aggression and Restlessness

There's this idea that everyone who gets dementia will turn angry or violent. That's not exactly true. Sure, it might happen to some—maybe around 30–50 percent—but not everyone is going to have these outbursts. And just like with anyone else, these reactions usually have a reason behind them. Aggression in people with dementia can spark from many things, and sometimes changing these things can help a lot:

- Physically: Aggression might come from changes in their brain because of the dementia or from side effects of medications. Sometimes it's from feeling paranoid or having hallucinations. Then again, it could be from stuff that annoys anybody—the noise, being in pain, hungry or thirsty, or just not clicking with someone.
- Psychologically: It's common for folks with dementia to feel scared and uncertain. When you're feeling lost or threatened, you might lash out. Plus, when caregivers don't get the approach quite right, it can lead to misunderstandings and frustration. Wanting to do things on their own but not being able to can also make a person irritable.
- Socially: Being lonely or bored, having personality clashes, or even well-meaning but clumsy actions by carers can set off anger. Imagine someone poking at you with a sponge on a stick in the shower. You'd probably be annoyed, right?

Remember, we're dealing with real people going through some really tough changes. A little understanding and a whole lot of patience can go a long way.

Sexual Disinhibition

Everyone has sexual feelings, both young and old, those with dementia and those without. But people with dementia may sometimes find it hard to control their sexual behaviors at the right times. They might act flirty or too close for comfort with others. In more severe cases, they might undress in public places, make unwanted sexual moves, or engage in sexual acts where others can see.

These actions are seen more often in men and can be ranked from most to least common as follows:

- Saying things that aren't appropriate
- Touching
- Fondling
- Stripping in public
- Being sexually forward
- Masturbating where others can see

The first two are usual and the least troubling; the rest can happen in about 10% of dementia cases and often worsen as the illness progresses.

Paranoia

Dementia can cause people to feel like they're being mistreated or to suspect others for no good reason. This paranoia might come from the damage dementia does to the brain or because the person gets confused easily. For example, a husband in a care home might think his wife left him for bad reasons if he can't remember her visits or recognize her photos.

Without thoughtful care, this fear can cause anxiety, upset, and even lead to angry outbursts. Carers can help by making sure they speak kindly and avoid restraining the person too much.

Mood Swings

Everyone experiences ups and downs—like feeling ready for the weekend or getting excited about a date. But in people with dementia, these mood changes can happen suddenly without any clear reason. In the blink of an eye, someone might go from chatting happily to walking around restlessly or crying. Small issues can cause big reactions, especially if this wasn't part of their personality before.

Noticing Functional Problems

Alongside the forgetfulness and emotional shifts in someone with dementia, difficulties with day-to-day tasks become more noticeable. Sure, we all have those moments when even simple tasks can seem tricky—like putting up a picture or changing a plug. However, for a person with dementia, it's common to struggle with these little things regularly because of the changes happening in their brain.

Cooking Complications

If you've whipped up a meal more times than you can count, chances are you can do it with your eyes closed, or at least without peeking at a recipe. Yet, those with dementia face a challenge that would leave even the famous chef Gordon Ramsay at a loss for words.

Typically, we rely on our memory to guide us through tasks like cooking without much thought, almost like we're on auto-pilot. But when someone has dementia, recalling these once-familiar steps becomes tough, turning even simple tasks, such as making beans on toast, into an ordeal. Short-term memory slips and timing troubles mean meals might end up burnt, undercooked, or forgotten until they're sprouting mold.

The New Hassle of Housekeeping

We all know someone whose home isn't exactly a beacon of cleanliness—think twice before eating off their floors. However, if an individual who used to take great pride in their clean home starts neglecting chores, it could signal something more concerning, like dementia, especially when paired with other behavior changes mentioned in this chapter. This might happen because they simply forget, lose interest mid-way, or lack the initiative—a key early sign of dementia.

For those naturally messy, their homes could spiral further into chaos. Picture visiting a once tidy gentleman now in his chair amidst a sea of dirty dishes and stale newspapers, with a makeshift toilet bucket as the centerpiece. Memory isn't just about reminiscing; it's fundamental to human life. Without the ability to remember, each moment feels isolated, leaving no past to reflect on or future to prepare for.

Unfortunately, dementia takes a toll on memory. There are two key types: short-term and long-term, plus an emotional memory—which, interestingly, remains intact despite dementia's progression. But it's the short-term memory that often falters first, affecting daily life in profound ways.

Chapter 3

Exploring the Various Forms of Dementia

In This Section:

- Uncover the primary forms of dementia.
- Recognize the unique symptoms of each type.
- Get a quick overview of treatment options.

Understanding dementia can be tricky—not only for those affected but for their loved ones as well. That's because dementia doesn't stem from just one cause; it's actually the result of several different conditions, each with its own set of distinct symptoms. Therefore, 'dementia' is a broad term that encompasses the impact that these various neurological issues have on a person's brain functions and their behavior.

In this section, we're going to get into the specifics of these conditions, taking a close look at the symptoms and the root causes, and the ongoing efforts to find treatments that can help manage these diseases. We'll kick things off with the most well-known and widespread form of dementia: Alzheimer's disease.

Alzheimer's Disease Explained

Alzheimer's disease is the most common kind of dementia and affects up to half a million people in the United States alone, which makes up most of the dementia cases there. It can impact adults at any age but is more usual as people grow older. The disease shows itself through certain symptoms and brain changes, helping doctors quickly identify it and suggest the best treatments to patients and their caregivers.

A Brief Look Into Alzheimer's History

Although Alzheimer's was officially discovered in 1910 by Dr. Alois Alzheimer – hence the name – the reality is a bit more complex. Historians note that:

- The condition was already known in the 1800s.
- The patient Dr. Alzheimer studied didn't quite match the modern criteria for Alzheimer's.
- It was actually Dr. Alzheimer's colleague, psychiatrist Dr. Emil Kraepelin, who named the disease after him.

Dr. Alzheimer's patient was a 51-year-old woman, Auguste D, in Frankfurt, Germany. She was admitted to a psychiatric hospital in 1901 for her memory issues, paranoia, aggressiveness, and auditory hallucinations. After she passed away in 1906, a post-mortem examination of her brain was presented at a scientific conference by Alzheimer, but it wasn't until three years later that Kraepelin termed the condition Alzheimer's disease.

Dementia in the 19th Century

Back in Dr. Alzheimer's time, 'dementia' was a broad term used to describe various conditions causing mental or social challenges, whether they were temporary and reversible, and no matter the age of the person. Now, we understand dementia as progressive and irreversible, gradually impairing memory, thinking, and the simple actions of daily life. Interestingly, Auguste D exhibited other symptoms like hallucinations that are not typical for an Alzheimer's diagnosis today, which makes her an unconventional case to define the disease.

Identifying a Unique Disease

Post-mortem observations of Auguste D's brain made it clear to the medical community that they were looking at a distinct disease. They found two key indicators:

- **Protein plaques**
- **Neurofibrillary tangles**

These abnormalities are due to proteins in the brain misfolding. However, Dr. Alzheimer wasn't the first to discover such brain changes. In fact, a Dr. Fuller from the USA had noted the tangles earlier, and European scientists had identified protein plaques in the late 1880s.

The Controversy of Naming the Disease

Labeling the disease "Alzheimer's" wasn't pointing out a new discovery. Historians believe that Dr. Kraepelin announced it as Alzheimer's disease partly to attract funding and publicity for his university department. Despite its contentious beginnings, the term Alzheimer's disease has remained and now refers to a specific neurodegenerative condition that doctors diagnose and manage using twenty-first-century medical knowledge.

Spotting the Early Signs of Alzheimer's Disease

Alzheimer's might have stirred up some debates in its early days, but nowadays, doctors are pretty certain about the signs that suggest someone might be developing the disease.

The signs of Alzheimer's tend to come on gradually. In fact, scientists think it could take up to 15 years from when Alzheimer's starts changing the brain to when a person shows all the classic symptoms.

Now, while there's a bit of symptom overlap between Alzheimer's and other kinds of dementia, each type has its own unique markers. Generally, these symptoms mess with:

- How people think and their memory
- Their mood and feelings
- The daily stuff they do

Thinking and Memory Issues

When most folks hear "dementia," they think about memory loss. I've got patients who visit me worried they're forgetting things or, in harder moments, say they're "losing their marbles." They just feel like something isn't right upstairs.

But Alzheimer's affects more than just memory – it scrambles a bunch of things beyond just recalling stuff.

Memory Basics

There are two types of memory to keep in mind:

Short-term memory is like your mental notepad. It helps you remember phone numbers, what you had for breakfast, and recent chats. It's not meant to hold onto things for long; information either fades or moves into long-term memory.

Long-term memory is your brain's huge storage room, keeping everything for a lifetime. From facts (like who grabbed the FA Cup in 1975) to sensations (the smell of your school's old lunchroom), it's all there. It's also where you keep how-tos like tying your shoes or riding a bike.

Memory Loss in Alzheimer's

With Alzheimer's, it's usually short-term memory that goes first. Someone might forget what they headed to the store for, not recall names of close friends, or regularly lose track of where they just put something.

On the flip side, long-term memories can stay sharp, making a person feel like they're back in their younger years. They might think they're much younger than they actually are or talk as though parents who have passed away are still around.

You might also notice they lose track of recent conversations. This can lead to repetitive questions that were just answered, or back-to-back phone calls discussing the same thing over. They may also keep telling the same stories because those are the memories they're sure about.

If someone you know is showing these signs, it's crucial to approach the situation with understanding and compassion. Alzheimer's can be a challenging road not just for those diagnosed but for their loved ones as well. Getting a proper medical evaluation early can help manage the symptoms and provide better care. Remember, you're not alone in this – there are resources and people ready to offer support every step of the way.

Alzheimer's disease affects more than just memory. It's like a ripple effect; as memory fades, so does the ability to handle what once were no-brainer tasks. Imagine feeling lost in your own neighborhood or forgetting your destination midway. That's the reality for those facing Alzheimer's.

Here's what else might happen:

- Familiar spaces become confusing, causing easy disorientation.
- It's common for individuals to wander off or leave their doors unlocked because they're in a rush and they forget.
- Misplacing items is a daily frustration — slippers in the fridge or even milk bottles in the oven are not as bizarre as they sound.
- Making decisions, especially regarding money and dressing appropriately for the weather, becomes a hurdle. It can lead to unnecessary purchases, confusion over change, or wearing a heavy coat on a sunny day.

Dealing with mood and emotions is challenging too. You might hear, "Dad's just not himself anymore," and it can be hard to recognize these signs, often dismissing them as simple moodiness when they are actually signs of this condition.

Mood swings can range from long-term sadness to rapid shifts from laughter to tears. Also, irritability, which can sometimes escalate to anger, is common, though it's important to remember that this can stem from fear or frustration, and not everyone experiences it the same way. Changes in emotion may lead to being suspicious or paranoid about those around them. There can be impatience or even inappropriate behavior due to a loss of social inhibitions, which can be startling for everyone.

With Alzheimer's, the ability to carry out these simple tasks dwindles. In the disease's later stages, some might even need help with eating or personal care. It's a tough road for anyone with Alzheimer's, as well as for those helping and caring for them. But understanding and patience can go a long way. Remember, it's about supporting individuals to manage their symptoms effectively while maintaining dignity and respect.

Understanding What Might Cause Alzheimer's Disease

Researchers haven't pinpointed a single cause of Alzheimer's disease, and it's likely that no single factor (like a unique virus or hazardous chemical) is to blame. Instead, the disease probably emerges from a combination of an individual's genes, lifestyle, and environment.

The Role of Genetics

There's quite a bit of evidence indicating that our genes may influence whether we develop Alzheimer's disease. Genetic influence varies between early-onset Alzheimer's, which affects people aged 30 to 60, and the more typical late-onset Alzheimer's that occurs after the age of 60.

Early-Onset Alzheimer's

This less common version of Alzheimer's makes up about 5% of all cases and appears to be hereditary due to gene mutations passed down from parents. Research is ongoing, and the list of genes involved is getting longer.

Late-Onset Alzheimer's

For those over 60 with Alzheimer's, a gene related to apolipoprotein E (APOE) is thought to be a contributor, along with potentially 20 other genes. APOE plays a role in breaking down beta-amyloid proteins inside brain cells. If there's an issue with the APOE gene, beta-amyloid may build up, leading to brain cell damage, a common sign of Alzheimer's.

Lifestyle Factors

It's well-supported that memory decline and brain function can be affected by decreased blood supply to brain cells. This can happen when blood vessels are harmed by what we're calling the unholy trinity:

- Smoking
- Eating poorly
- Not exercising enough

Throw in obesity, heavy drinking, diabetes, and unchecked high blood pressure, and you've got the perfect storm for Alzheimer's disease. Another risk factor could be not having enough social interaction, since isolation and mental inactivity may also contribute to developing Alzheimer's.

Environmental Concerns

The concern here isn't about climate change or rainforest loss, though those shouldn't be overlooked. For Alzheimer's, we're talking about exposure to pesticides like DDT and certain nitrogen-based fertilizers. Scientists think these might increase our risk of getting Alzheimer's. The connection isn't clear-cut yet, but our environment could be another piece of the puzzle. While researchers work fervently to uncover the mysteries of Alzheimer's, knowing these risk factors gives us a clearer image of what we're up against.

If you or someone you love is facing symptoms that might suggest Alzheimer's disease, it's important to understand that pinpointing this condition isn't as straightforward as completing a single test. Unfortunately, we can't rely on just one blood test, scan, or questionnaire to confirm a diagnosis. This can be frustrating because it leaves those experiencing symptoms of dementia in a kind of medical gray area.

However, there's a silver lining. Doctors have several tests at their disposal that, when combined, help make the picture clearer. Think of it like putting together a puzzle—each test adds a piece, gradually forming the complete image. Though it's worth noting that sometimes the emerging picture might shift as new information comes to light.

Rule Out Other Causes

Before jumping to conclusions, it's essential to rule out other health issues that mimic dementia. Since no blood test exists specifically for Alzheimer's, your doctor will start with general blood tests to cross off other possibilities. These tests check for conditions such as:

- Anemia
- Thyroid problems
- Diabetes
- Imbalances in electrolytes like sodium and potassium
- Calcium levels
- Vitamin deficiencies, especially B12 and folic acid

Urine Tests

Something as simple as a urinary tract infection can cause severe confusion in older adults. This state of confusion doesn't usually last—as with dementia—but ensuring that the trouble isn't due to an infection is a crucial first step before moving on to more detailed examinations.

Brain Scans

Ultimately, brain scans may provide the missing piece to confirm an Alzheimer's diagnosis. Based on symptoms, doctors decide between several types of scans:

CT Scans

A CT (Computerized Tomography) scan is quite common. It involves lying in a machine that might remind you of a big doughnut while safe x-ray beams pass through your brain. A computer then uses these beams to create slice-by-slice images of the brain, allowing doctors to examine it from different angles.

MRI Scans

An MRI (Magnetic Resonance Imaging) scan uses magnetic fields and radio waves to take pictures of your brain. Much like with CT scans, the images are reviewed in sections, offering detailed views of what's going on inside.

MRI scans are particularly useful for checking out the brain's blood vessels.

SPECT Scans

SPECT (Single Photon Emission Computed Tomography) scans are a bit more specialized and use gamma-rays to create a 3D image of your brain. It's a good way to analyze brain metabolism and detect abnormalities common in Alzheimer's, boasting over 70% sensitivity. However, SPECT scans are pricier and not as widely available, often reserved for cases where other methods haven't given clear answers, or they are available through private healthcare at a cost. Alzheimer's-specific changes, like decreased overall brain size and notable shrinkage in memory-associated areas like the hippocampus, can become evident through these scans.

Diagnosing Alzheimer's is a detailed process that involves piecing together information from various tests. While it may feel overwhelming, rest assured that modern medicine offers tools to guide you and your loved ones through this challenging time with clarity and support.

When it comes to treatment options, it's essential to acknowledge that there is currently no cure for Alzheimer's disease. However, there are four approved medications that can help slow down the progression of the disease and mitigate some of the cognitive symptoms:

- Donepezil,
- Galantamine,
- Rivastigmine,
- Memantine.

These medications aim to stabilize the symptoms, and many patients have noticed some improvements within the first six months of treatment. In addition to medication, there are behavioral and psychological strategies available to address the more challenging symptoms that might emerge as the disease advances.

It's vital to be realistic about expectations with Alzheimer's disease. Sadly, the condition is incurable, and symptoms will worsen over time. The rate at which the disease progresses can vary significantly from person to person; after being diagnosed, some people live anywhere from 5 to 20 years, depending greatly on the disease's severity and the level and type of care they receive.

Chapter 4

Vascular Dementia

Vascular dementia is the second-leading type of dementia, with about 20% of all dementia cases in the US. More than 100,000 people are living with it.

Vascular dementia is more than a simple memory issue; it's a complex condition that impacts various aspects of daily life. One of these is communication. Much like a disrupted phone line, vascular dementia can scramble messages in the brain, making it difficult for individuals to express themselves clearly. For instance, you may find your loved one struggling to find the right words during a conversation or repeating the same questions.

Vascular dementia, a common form of cognitive decline, is often misunderstood and overlooked. It's like trying to get out of a maze without a map; the mind's pathways become blocked and twisted, leading to confusion and memory loss. This phenomenon is no longer rare as our population ages, becoming an increasingly prevalent issue. Yet, hope isn't lost; recent studies suggest that understanding and managing vascular dementia can significantly improve quality of life. While Alzheimer's disease is widely recognized, vascular dementia stays in its shadow. However, it is the second most common type of dementia after Alzheimer's. Its unique characteristic comes from its cause - it results from conditions that block or reduce blood flow to various parts of the brain, depriving them of essential oxygen and nutrients.

Vascular dementia can manifest in subtle ways before progressing to more severe symptoms. Early signs may include slight forgetfulness or difficulty concentrating. As it progresses, however, these symptoms can escalate into severe memory loss, confusion about time or place, and even physical symptoms like difficulty walking or speaking clearly.

Understanding the root cause of vascular dementia provides valuable insight into its prevention and management. Conditions such as stroke or heart disease often precede this form of dementia. Thus, focusing on cardiovascular health becomes crucial not only for your heart but also for your brain. A study published in The Lancet Neurology found that controlling high blood pressure significantly reduced the risk of developing mild cognitive impairment and dementia. This underscores the importance of maintaining good cardiovascular health as a preventive measure against vascular dementia. Continuing to delve into the world of vascular dementia, it's important to understand that while there is now no cure, there are ways to manage its symptoms and slow its progression. Medications used for Alzheimer's can sometimes help with the cognitive symptoms of vascular dementia. Additionally, lifestyle changes such as regular exercise, a healthy diet, and controlling blood pressure can make a significant difference.

Vascular dementia is not just a person's battle; it's a collective fight. Its impact ripples through families and communities, reshaping lives in its wake. Yet, understanding it can be the first step to turning the tide, reminding us that even in the face of adversity, the human spirit stays unyielding.

It started subtly for Martha, a retired schoolteacher. She would forget where she placed her eyeglasses or miss an appointment now and then. Her family attributed these incidents to normal aging until one day, Martha got lost on her way home from the grocery store, a route she had been taking for decades.

A consultation with Martha's doctor led to a series of tests that concluded she was suffering from vascular dementia. The diagnosis was heartbreaking for her family, but it also provided clarity and guidance on how best to support their beloved matriarch. Just like Martha, many people may experience symptoms of vascular dementia without recognizing them as such. This chapter aims to help you identify these signs early on and equip you with strategies to manage this condition.

Vascular dementia is a condition that causes changes in thinking skills, which occur because of brain damage from impaired blood flow to your brain. A study published in the journal "Stroke" highlighted that unlike Alzheimer's, where memory loss is typically the first symptom, vascular dementia often begins with noticeable problems in executing tasks or understanding concepts.

According to this study, people with vascular dementia may experience difficulties with problem-solving or focused thinking more prominently than memory issues at first. This could manifest as struggling with planning and organizing or making decisions. They might also have trouble following a series of steps (like cooking a meal), controlling their bladder, or walking or moving steadily.

It's not uncommon for people with VaD to experience mood changes such as depression or apathy. Physical symptoms may include weakness on one side of the body or difficulty walking - both potential indicators of underlying cerebrovascular disease.

A study published in the Journal of the American Medical Association (JAMA) found that intensive blood pressure control significantly reduces the risk of mild cognitive impairment, a precursor to dementia. The researchers discovered that by keeping systolic blood pressure (the top number in a reading) below 120, as opposed to the standard 140, the risk of mild cognitive impairment was reduced by 19%. This suggests that maintaining a healthy blood pressure could be a key strategy in preventing vascular dementia. Always remember that early detection can lead to better outcomes; therefore, staying vigilant about any changes in cognitive abilities is crucial.

As vascular dementia progresses, symptoms can become more apparent. These might include physical weakness or paralysis on one side of the body, inability to understand or formulate speech (known as aphasia), and problems with seeing things in three dimensions.

Moreover, another key difference pointed out by researchers is the pattern of cognitive decline. In Alzheimer's disease, this decline tends to be gradual and steady while in vascular dementia it can often be 'step-wise'. That means a person may stay at one level for some time then suddenly drop down rather than gradually deteriorate.

Therefore, keeping an eye out for progressive symptoms can aid timely medical intervention and treatment.

Pay attention not just to memory loss but also difficulties with task execution and sudden drops in cognitive function – these could be signs pointing towards vascular dementia rather than other forms of this condition.

According to a study published in The Lancet Neurology, vascular dementia progresses in seven stages. Understanding these stages can help you provide better care for someone with this condition and prepare for what's ahead.

1. No Cognitive Decline: In this stage, individuals experience no significant memory problems or other symptoms of dementia.

2. Very Mild Cognitive Decline: This stage may involve slight memory problems or losing things around the house, although not enough to interfere with daily life or be noticeable to friends or family.

3. Mild Cognitive Decline: Early-stage vascular dementia might involve mild changes in cognitive functions that are noticeable to the person affected and possibly to family members close to them.

4. Moderate Cognitive Decline: In this stage, clear-cut symptoms are apparent, such as forgetting recent events and having trouble managing finances or traveling alone outside the home.

5. Moderately Severe Cognitive Decline: During mid-stage vascular dementia, people may need assistance with many day-to-day activities like dressing or eating.

6. Severe Cognitive Decline (Middle Dementia): Memory continues to worsen, personality changes may take place and individuals need extensive help with daily activities.

7. Very Severe Cognitive Decline (Late Dementia): In the final stage of this disease, individuals lose the ability to respond to their environment, carry on a conversation and control movement.

The progression through these stages is different for everyone – it can take years – but understanding them helps manage expectations about what might happen next.

Regular medical check-ups play a crucial role in managing vascular dementia. They allow doctors to watch the disease's progression and adjust treatment plans accordingly. Regular screenings for high blood pressure, high cholesterol, and diabetes—conditions that can increase the risk of vascular dementia—are also important.

The main issue with vascular dementia is blood flow problems. When the brain cells don't get enough blood, they don't receive enough oxygen and start to die. Losing a lot of brain cells this way can cause dementia.

It's important to figure out what's causing the blood flow problems. They could be due to:

- Strokes
- Transient ischemic attacks (TIAs), also known as "mini-strokes" that get better after 24 hours
- Narrowing arteries from a build-up of plaque (atherosclerosis)
- Bleeding in the brain (hemorrhage)
- Heart failure

Binswanger's disease is a specific form of vascular dementia linked to damage to tiny blood vessels in deeper parts of the brain. Unlike other forms, Binswanger's mainly impacts the brain's white matter. It's sometimes referred to as "hardening of the arteries" and it also leads to the loss of brain cells. This condition is more common in people in their 50s and 60s and it gets worse as they age.

Spotting the symptoms of vascular dementia is key. They are similar to Alzheimer's but can include other signs like weakness on one side of the body – telltale signs of strokes. Unlike Alzheimer's, vascular dementia often moves forward in steps – each new stroke or TIA can cause a sudden decline in cognitive abilities.

However, not everyone experiences these sudden changes. Some people, especially those with Binswanger's disease, may see a steady decline, similar to Alzheimer's progression.

You watch as your mother, a woman once so sharp and quick-witted, struggles to remember the name of her favorite book. It's not just simple forgetfulness; she frequently has trouble with directions, often losing her train of thought mid-conversation. More alarmingly, these episodes are accompanied by occasional headaches and unsteady gait.

A visit to her doctor draws attention to her high blood pressure and history of mini-strokes. The physician suggests that these symptoms might be indicative of vascular dementia (VaD).

Many older adults exhibit early signs of VaD that are often misunderstood or overlooked.

When symptoms suggestive of VaD arise, it's essential to seek a comprehensive medical evaluation. Your healthcare provider will likely start with a thorough check of medical history followed by physical and neurological examinations.

These evaluations help rule out other potential causes and assess risk factors such as hypertension, diabetes, smoking habits or history of stroke – common culprits in the development of VaD.

Science shows that diagnosing vascular dementia, like other types of dementia, involves a series of tests including physical examinations, cognitive and neuropsychological tests, brain imaging scans, and blood tests. However, what sets vascular dementia apart is its unique cause - it's often because of reduced or blocked blood flow in the brain that can be detected through specific imaging techniques.

A study published in the Journal of Alzheimer's Disease suggests that MRI scans are particularly effective in identifying changes in the brain associated with vascular dementia. These scans can reveal abnormalities such as infarcts or strokes, white matter lesions and overall brain atrophy which are common indicators of this type of dementia.

Moreover, emotional and behavioral assessments play a crucial role too. Vascular dementia patients may exhibit mood swings, depression or apathy which differ from other forms of dementia where memory loss is more prominent.

To assess cognitive function, healthcare providers may use structured tests that measure memory, attention, language skills and problem-solving abilities. These tests help identify areas of cognitive impairment and determine their severity.

Understanding the early signs of Vascular Dementia is crucial for timely intervention. The sooner VaD is diagnosed, the sooner necessary lifestyle modifications can be made to slow its progression and better manage its symptoms.

Furthermore, remember that while dealing with any form of Dementia can be challenging; there are ways to manage Vascular Dementia better by focusing on controlling cardiovascular risk factors such as high blood pressure & cholesterol levels.

By following this guide to diagnosis, you're taking a significant step towards effectively managing Vascular Dementia in your loved ones or yourself.

Other symptoms to watch for include:

- Declining thinking skills and memory loss
- Difficulty walking or keeping balance
- Personality changes, which can include aggression
- Feeling depressed
- Seeing or hearing things that aren't there
- Needing to urinate more often, which may come with difficulty controlling it

- The older you get, the higher your risk.
- High blood pressure is the biggest bad guy when it comes to your blood vessels.
- Heart troubles, including heart attacks, chest pain from not enough blood flow, iffy heart valves that might create small clots, and a kind of uneven heartbeat called atrial fibrillation.
- When your blood vessels get stiff and narrow, which doctors call atherosclerosis.
- Diabetes, especially when it's not kept in check.
- Smoking – just steer clear, okay?
- Genetic issues, like a family condition that's got a long name but goes by CADASIL for short.

About CADASIL

CADASIL is rare, thankfully. A glitch on gene number 19 causes it, and it's something you can find in about 1 in 200,000 people, hitting men and women alike. If one of your parents has it, you've got a 50/50 shot at inheriting this gene.

Usually, folks start noticing something's up in their 20s with nasty migraine headaches with visual weirdness like seeing squiggly lines, getting dizzy, not liking bright lights, or hearing ringing. In their 30s, those with CADASIL might start having strokes or mini-strokes and could begin showing signs of dementia. Sadly, over the next couple of decades, these symptoms worsen, and most people with CADASIL pass away too early, in their 50s.

Brain scans can spot CADASIL, but finding it early doesn't mean there's a cure. The best we can do is manage the symptoms as they come.

Understanding the Tests for Vascular Dementia

When doctors suspect someone might have vascular dementia, they begin many of the same steps as they would for Alzheimer's disease. First, they gather the person's full medical history, checking if there have been any strokes or mini-strokes (called TIAs), and looking at urinary or movement issues. The doctor will also examine the person carefully, paying close attention to blood pressure and heart health, and checking any neurological concerns, especially if there's a history of stroke.

Blood, urine, and memory or cognitive tests are part of this initial check-up. But for vascular dementia, brain scans like a CT or MRI, which you might have heard about in the Alzheimer's section, take on a starring role. These scans can spot strokes, TIAs, or any issues with blood vessels. If the scans reveal changes in the brain's blood vessels, the doctor may order additional scans of the patient's blood flow. They'll use special types of ultrasound scanners to peek at blood flow in the neck's arteries and through the heart. Discovering issues here could signal a higher risk of more strokes or TIAs, but some of these problems can be treated.

Exploring Treatment Options

Unfortunately, there's no cure for vascular dementia, just like Alzheimer's. But there's still hope - some treatments can slow down its progress, halt further damage, and prevent more strokes or TIAs.

Doctors will coach patients on healthier lifestyles and may prescribe various medications. They'll tell patients to quit smoking, switch to a diet that is low in fat and high in fiber, reduce alcohol intake, and exercise if possible.

Medication focuses on:

- Managing blood pressure.
- Keeping cholesterol levels in check.
- Controlling diabetes to maintain ideal blood sugar levels.
- Using blood thinners to help avoid more strokes or TIAs.

Sometimes, drugs typically used for Alzheimer's disease might be prescribed if the patient seems to show signs of both conditions. A study published in The Lancet Neurology suggests that controlling cardiovascular risk factors may be a key strategy in preventing and treating vascular dementia. This includes managing high blood pressure, maintaining healthy cholesterol levels, quitting smoking, exercising regularly, eating a balanced diet and controlling diabetes if present.

Medication plays a critical role in treating vascular dementia symptoms. While there's currently no cure for vascular dementia, certain medications can significantly help manage its symptoms and improve quality of life. One such medication is donepezil, often prescribed to help boost brain function and slow cognitive decline. Always talk to your healthcare provider before starting any new medication regimen. Research from the Journal of Neurology states that donepezil shows consistent benefits on measures of cognitive function, activities of daily living scales.""

Remember that adherence is key when it comes to medication management — take them as prescribed by your doctor. Unlike Alzheimer's disease where medication can only slow down the progression of symptoms but not stop them completely; for vascular dementia - prevention is possible. A healthier lifestyle can significantly reduce the risk of strokes which are often responsible for this type of dementia.

A scientific study published in the Journal of Neurology Neurosurgery & Psychiatry suggests that physical activity can have a protective effect against vascular cognitive impairment. Regular exercise increases blood flow to the brain and stimulates the growth of new neurons. Therefore, incorporating regular physical activities such as walking or swimming into your daily routine could help slow down the progression of vascular dementia.

In addition to lifestyle changes and medications to manage underlying conditions like hypertension or diabetes; cognitive rehabilitation might also be useful for people with vascular dementia. Cognitive rehabilitation involves strategies to improve cognitive functions such as memory and attention. A Cochrane review shows that cognitive stimulation therapy (CST), which involves engaging in a range of activities and discussions (usually in a group setting), has been shown to improve cognition in people with mild to moderate dementia. This might include memory training exercises or problem-solving tasks.

Emotionally, it's important for those suffering from any form of dementia to receive psychological support. According to an article published in Aging & Mental Health journal, mindfulness-based stress reduction (MBSR) has been found effective at reducing anxiety and depression symptoms among caregivers for people with dementia. Hence, offering emotional support not just for patients but also their caregivers is vital.

Behavioral changes are another challenge faced by people with vascular dementia. The National Institute on Aging recommends tailored interventions based on understanding what triggers certain behaviors - this could be discomfort or environmental factors like noise level.

What sets treatment apart for vascular dementia compared to other forms is its focus on preventing further damage because of cerebrovascular issues. According to Mayo Clinic experts, controlling key health factors — especially high blood pressure — can significantly slow down progression of this disease.

Remember: each person's journey with dementia will look different based on their person circumstances. It's always important to talk to healthcare professionals who understand your specific situation before making any major decisions about treatment or care. Recent advancements in medical science have provided us with promising strategies to manage and even slow down the progression of this condition. Healthy lifestyle changes, cognitive therapy, and certain medications have shown potential in reducing the symptoms of vascular dementia. Scientific research has shown that while all forms of dementia share common symptoms such as memory loss, confusion, and difficulty with thinking and problem-solving, the treatment approach for vascular dementia differs significantly from other types of dementia like Alzheimer's disease.

Being Realistic About Vascular Dementia

The future for someone with vascular dementia isn't certain. But we know from the numbers that about one-third of those diagnosed--sadly--may pass away from its complications. Another third might die from strokes linked to their cerebrovascular disease. Those with any type of vascular dementia will likely face a reduced lifespan.

It's a tough journey, but understanding what to expect and the available support can offer some comfort and direction. The medical team is there every step of the way to help manage the condition with professionalism and care.

Chapter 5

Understanding Mixed Dementia as an Increasingly Common Condition

Mixed dementia emerges as the third leading type of dementia and is especially more prevalent as individuals grow older. I remember the day I first noticed it, as clearly as if it were yesterday. My father, a man of great intellect and humor, was searching for a word - not an unusual occurrence for anyone really. But this was different; he couldn't recall the word 'birthday'. It seemed like such an insignificant thing then; little did I know it was our first introduction to an uninvited guest that would change our lives forever - mixed dementia.

Mixed dementia is like an unwelcome visitor who shows up at your door one day and refuses to leave. You can't reason with it or convince it to go away. It just settles in, making itself comfortable while slowly eroding the person you love right before your eyes.

As author Robert Brault once said, "Life becomes easier when you learn to accept the apology you never got." This book is my move through accepting that unspoken apology from dcmcntia for stealing away parts of my beloved father bit by bit.

In this chapter we'll explore what mixed dementia is exactly and how it differs from other types of dementia. We'll delve into its symptoms and progression – which often seem shrouded in mystery until they're happening right under your nose.

We will also talk about various coping mechanisms – not only for those living with this condition but also for their loved ones acting as caregivers. Because let's face it - watching someone you love grapple with mixed dementia can feel like being stuck on a rollercoaster ride that only goes down.

In telling our story, I hope to shine some light on this often misunderstood condition and provide comfort to others walking this path too.

It started subtly enough; Dad forgetting simple words here and there soon turned into him forgetting events altogether. One chilling winter morning he looked at me, his eyes vacant, and I realized he didn't recognize his own daughter. That was the moment our fight began in earnest against this uninvited guest.

I'll never forget that feeling of helplessness, like standing on a beach watching a tidal wave approach with nowhere to run. But as we journeyed through this together, I learned that even amidst the chaos and heartache, there can be moments of clarity and joy too.

So come along with me as we pull back the curtain on mixed dementia. It's not an easy journey by any means, but it's one that needs to be shared. As we navigate these waters together, remember - you are not alone. And sometimes, knowing that is half the battle won.

The Coexistence of Multiple Dementia Types

The term 'mixed dementia' refers to the presence of not just one, but at least two types of dementia processes in a person's brain simultaneously. However, it is important to note that having mixed dementia doesn't imply the individual suffers from 'twice' the effects. Commonly, people with this condition have Alzheimer's disease alongside vascular dementia. Alzheimer's can also co-occur with Lewy body disease, and in rarer instances, individuals have been reported to have all three conditions—Alzheimer's, vascular dementia, and Lewy body disease—at once.

Despite technological advancements in medical tests aimed to diagnose dementia, achieving an exact diagnosis remains an ongoing challenge. Symptoms often overlap, making it difficult for healthcare professionals to distinguish and offer a precise diagnosis for each case. Consequently, it's believed that there might be a larger segment of individuals living with mixed dementia than those currently diagnosed by the medical community.

Identifying Mixed Dementia Symptoms

Recognizing symptoms of mixed dementia can be complex because they derive from the interaction of different underlying dementias. Unlike the simplicity of identifying symptoms specific to single forms of dementia, mixed dementia symptoms do not present in an isolated or quantifiable manner.

To illustrate this complexity, picture a unique analogy related to food. When visualizing symptoms, instead of seeing a neat plate with separated components—like a Sunday roast where you can distinctly identify each flavor—the symptoms of mixed dementia are akin to a stew. Ingredients—representative of various symptoms—are intermixed, resulting in a less distinctive taste, where individual components are not as easily recognisable. The most notable symptoms associated with mixed dementia are those present in Alzheimer's disease and vascular dementia. These could also encompass symptoms of related cardiovascular conditions, including heart diseases, strokes, or transient ischemic attacks (TIAs). The presentation and intensity of symptoms will vary from person to person.

Considering the Risk Factors

Mixed dementia arises from the combination of different pathological processes within the brain, typically involving the pathologies seen in Alzheimer's disease and circulatory conditions like arteriosclerosis or stroke-induced damages. Understanding these risk factors and the ways they contribute to the development of mixed dementia is a critical part of managing and responding to the condition.

Navigating Diagnostic Tests

Upon consulting a doctor for memory concerns or cognitive impairments, individuals typically undergo an array of basic tests analogous to those used for diagnosing Alzheimer's disease. These initial assessments aim to confirm the presence of dementia and then further narrow down the specific type or types involved. Because mixed dementia presents a conglomeration of symptoms, often a diagnosis is reached upon observing a blend of both dementia signs.

In-depth diagnostic measures, such as brain scans, are instrumental in pinpointing features consistent with both Alzheimer's disease and vascular dementia. Results might show a generalized reduction in brain cells, particularly within the temporal lobe and hippocampal region, or they might depict evidence of stroke, TIA occurrences, or generalized arteriosclerosis. These imaging results, combined with symptom assessment, support the identification of mixed dementia.

In summary, understanding mixed dementia as a compounded condition that involves various dementia processes is key in managing its symptoms and providing targeted care for those affected. With ongoing research and improved diagnostics, clearer insights will hopefully emerge, facilitating better support and outcomes for individuals living with this intricate form of dementia.

Exploring Treatment Options for Mixed Dementia

Sadly, when it comes to mixed dementia, we are faced with the same reality as its individual components—currently, there is no known cure for this complex condition. Mixed dementia is a term that refers to the condition when an individual is experiencing the symptoms of more than one type of dementia simultaneously; most commonly Alzheimer's disease paired with vascular dementia.

Despite the absence of a cure, there is a silver lining in the realm of treatment. Certain medications that have been developed to treat Alzheimer's disease appear to show positive effects in managing some symptoms of mixed dementia. These medications include donepezil, galantamine, and rivastigmine. They are primarily designed to alleviate cognitive symptoms, such as memory loss and confusion, which can bring some relief and an improvement in quality of life for those affected.

For those suffering from mixed dementia, a multi-faceted approach to treatment can be beneficial. Ensuring that someone with this condition receives comprehensive care that targets the vascular aspect is crucial. Effective management includes, but is not limited to, the vigilant control of blood pressure. Keeping blood pressure within the recommended range is essential in possibly slowing the dementia's progression. Additionally, lowering cholesterol levels through diet, medication, or a combination of both is another proactive step in managing the risks associated with vascular factors. Preventive measures against future strokes, heart attacks, or transient ischemic attacks (TIAs) are also a major component of the care plan. Each of these can potentially exacerbate the complications associated with vascular dementia, therefore making dedicated prevention efforts critical.

Realistic Expectations Regarding Prognosis of Mixed Dementia

It's important to face the prognosis of mixed dementia with a realistic mindset, as this diagnosis alters expectations for the future. The prognosis for those with mixed dementia often parallels that of individuals with vascular diseases. Generally, the life expectancy of patients with mixed dementia may be shorter. This outlook is not only due to the neurodegenerative nature of the illnesses involved but also due to the potential complications arising from the vascular components.

The progression of mixed dementia can vary significantly from person to person and is influenced by a myriad of factors, including overall health, age at diagnosis, and the severity of the vascular disease. While some may experience a gradual decline, others could have more rapid changes in their cognitive and physical abilities. Being informed about the nature of mixed dementia and understanding the available treatments can empower patients and their caregivers to make knowledgeable decisions about care. Support systems, including healthcare teams and caregiver resources, play a pivotal role in managing the illness. It's also beneficial to engage with support groups and online forums where sharing experiences can provide comfort and practical advice.

In summary, while mixed dementia presents a challenging path, with attentive medical care focused on the underlying issues and symptomatic relief, those affected can lead a life marked by dignity and as much engagement as possible. It's essential to continue monitoring and adapting treatment strategies under professional guidance to ensure the best possible outcomes.

Chapter 6

Understanding Fronto-Temporal Dementia

Fronto-temporal dementia (FTD) stands out as a very specific and distinctive form of dementia that impacts certain regions of the brain. This characteristic gives it its name as well as dictates the patterns of symptoms witnessed in patients. It distinguishes itself from other common forms of dementia, not just in terms of prevalence – as it's considered to be among the rarest – but also because of its tendency to manifest within family lines, suggesting a genetic link.

A Tale of Two Minds

John was a lively man, full of energy and enthusiasm for life. His wife, Mary, brought him to a neurologist because she had noticed some changes in his behavior that concerned her.

John had always been the life of the party - charming, witty, and charismatic. But recently he had become withdrawn and uninterested in social activities. He would sit quietly at parties where he used to be the center of attention. More concerning were his moments of confusion and forgetfulness - misplacing keys or forgetting appointments.

At first glance, it might be stress or depression. But as we dig deeper into John's history and symptoms, a different picture begins to emerge.

One day Mary called the neurologist in distress. John had left their home without telling her where he was going and hadn't returned for several hours. She found him sitting alone on a park bench across town with no recollection of how he got there or why he left home.

That's when they suspected frontotemporal dementia (FTD). FTD is not like Alzheimer's disease where memory loss is prominent; instead, it affects personality, behavior, language abilities while leaving memory relatively intact initially.

They ran tests – brain scans showed shrinkage in frontal and temporal lobes confirming their worst fears - Frontotemporal Dementia it was!

Over time John's condition worsened. He became more confused about time and place; his once sparkling conversation turned into disjointed phrases making little sense; even recognizing faces became difficult for him.

It was heartbreaking to watch this vibrant man slowly fade away before our eyes but what struck me most was Mary's resilience during these trying times.

Mary never gave up on John despite all odds against them! She patiently reminded him about dates or events; she took over household chores which were once his domain; she became his voice when he couldn't express himself.

Through Mary, we learn that while FTD may rob a person of their cognitive abilities, it doesn't take away the essence of who they are. John was still there - behind the confusion and memory loss - and Mary's love for him never wavered. As we close this chapter on John's story, remember that frontotemporal dementia is not just a medical condition but a human experience. And as healthcare providers or caregivers our role goes beyond treating symptoms – we must also care for the person beneath them. Just like a sudden rainstorm can disrupt a sunny afternoon picnic, frontotemporal dementia (FTD) can abruptly turn the lives of people and their families upside down. This condition, which is often misdiagnosed or misunderstood, can change your loved one into an unrecognizable person, altering their personality and behavior in profound ways.

Frontotemporal dementia plays a pivotal role in the field of neurodegenerative diseases. First off, it's unique in that it typically affects people at a younger age than most forms of dementia, often striking in the prime of life. For instance, while Alzheimer's usually becomes obvious in your late 60s, FTD often shows up when a person is in their 40s or 50s but can also affect younger or older people.

Secondly, unlike other forms of dementia that primarily affect memory, FTD primarily affects areas of the brain associated with personality, behavior, and language. This means someone suffering from FTD might forget the name of their favorite song or struggle to remember important dates, but they'll also show drastic changes in their character. A once gentle and patient individual might become aggressive and impatient, causing distress for both themselves and their loved ones. It's often misdiagnosed as a psychiatric problem or as Alzheimer's disease because of its unique symptoms which include drastic changes in personality, strange behaviors or difficulty with producing or comprehending language.

A study published in The Lancet Neurology found that people with FTD showed significant changes in their social behavior and personal conduct long before they received their diagnosis. They lost interest in their usual activities, acted out of character, made impulsive decisions or neglected their personal responsibilities.

As FTD progresses, people may struggle with basic tasks like planning and organizing. They may also become socially withdrawn or display inappropriate behaviors. It's important to remember that these changes are a result of the disease and not the person's choice.

Lastly, FTD underscores the importance of early diagnosis for effective management. Because its symptoms can be so varied and its onset so early, it's often mistaken for psychiatric problems or other neurological disorders. However, timely recognition of signs and symptoms can lead to suitable interventions that may improve quality of life. The stages of frontotemporal dementia are:

1: It typically begins subtly with mild personality changes or trouble with language, and gradually advances to more severe cognitive impairments. The progression of FTD can be divided into early, middle, and late stages.

2: In the early stage of frontotemporal dementia, individuals may exhibit subtle changes in personality and behavior. They might become less empathetic towards others or start behaving impulsively. Difficulty with language may also occur at this stage - for instance, struggling to find the right words during conversation or forgetting the names of everyday objects.

3: As frontotemporal dementia progresses into the middle stage, symptoms become more noticeable. Individuals may have significant difficulty with speech and understanding language. Behavioral changes often intensify as well; they might show poor judgment, act out socially inappropriate behaviors or show a lack of interest in personal hygiene.

4: The late stage of frontotemporal dementia is characterized by severe cognitive impairment. At this point, individuals may need assistance with daily activities such as eating, dressing and bathing. Communication becomes very challenging because of advanced language difficulties. In some cases, physical symptoms like muscle weakness or coordination problems may also develop.

5: It's important to note that not everyone will experience all these stages in a linear fashion; the progression of FTD varies greatly from person to person based on factors like overall health status and subtype of FTD diagnosed. Regular check-ups with healthcare professionals are crucial in managing this condition effectively.

Frontotemporal dementia is not just a medical condition; it's a life-altering journey that demands patience, understanding, and resilience from everyone involved. It challenges our concept of identity and forces us to redefine our relationships with those affected. Yet, it also offers an opportunity for growth, as we learn to navigate the storm and find new ways to connect with our loved ones. As we further delve into FTD, remember this: while the rain may disrupt our picnic, it doesn't mean we can't enjoy the beauty of the rainbow that follows.

Delving Into What Sets FTD Apart

Unlike other types of dementia which can occur in the later stages of life, FTD often emerges much earlier. It is frequently diagnosed in individuals under the age of 65, and it's not uncommon for people in their mid-forties to exhibit symptoms. What makes FTD particularly unusual is its focus on two specific areas of the brain: the frontal lobes, located at the front, and the temporal lobes, situated on either side of the brain.

Arnold Pick, a psychiatrist, first recognized FTD as a distinct condition way back in 1892. For a considerable period, it was referred to as Pick's disease, named after its discoverer, which highlights its individuality among cognitive disorders.

Identifying Symptoms of Fronto-Temporal Dementia

FTD manifests in three primary types, each with unique symptoms influenced by the particular areas of the brain affected.

Behavioral Variant FTD

If one is grappling with this variant of FTD, they might encounter a variety of symptoms:

- A significant loss of inhibitions may lead to socially peculiar or inappropriate actions, often without the usual tact most people intuitively maintain.
- A general disinterest in interpersonal relationships and activities that were once enjoyable, not linked to typical signs of depression.

- Diminished capacity for empathy and sympathy towards others.
- Emergence of compulsive behaviors, such as a propensity to accumulate items unnecessarily (hoarding) or an obsession with rituals like strict timekeeping.
- A marked change in eating habits, which may include overindulgence in junk foods, heightened cravings for sweets, or increased consumption of alcohol and cigarettes.

Interestingly, one of the key contrasting features of this type of dementia is that memory loss, frequently associated with other forms of dementia, isn't predominantly profound.

Language Variants of FTD

Two forms of FTD result in disruption to standard communication:

- **Progressive Non-Fluent Aphasia**: Here, a sufferer's speech may become labored and hesitant with evident stuttering. They can struggle with word pronunciation and simplification of grammatical structure, often skipping connecting words such as 'and', 'the', or 'to'.
- **Semantic FTD**: In this case, communication may appear smooth yet hindered by the individual's inability to recall specific words or names. The affected person may have to resort to general terms like 'thing' or 'animal' when more precise words evade them.

The Incidence of Overlapping Syndromes

A curious subset of individuals, around 20 percent of those affected by FTD, will concurrently develop a motor disorder. Conditions such as motor neurone disease or progressive supranuclear palsy could be accompanying issues. Consequently, a person may be coping with dementia and the distinguishing features of their specific type of FTD while also dealing with physical manifestations like muscle weakness or involuntary muscle twitches in various parts of their body. Understanding and recognizing the nuances of fronto-temporal dementia is critical for diagnosis and management. For families and caregivers, knowledge about the specific variants and the implications it might have on the motor functions can be invaluable in providing appropriate care and support for loved ones dealing with this unique condition.

Exploring treatment possibilities is a vital step after a diagnosis of any dementia-related illness. This is especially true for Frontotemporal Dementia (FTD), a condition that, unfortunately, the medical community continues to grapple with. Despite ongoing research and advancements in our understanding of dementia, an effective treatment for FTD remains elusive. The condition, as it stands, has no known cure, and methods to impede its progression haven't been discovered yet.

Medications currently on the market that are traditionally used to manage Alzheimer's disease, another form of dementia, are not suitable for individuals with FTD. In fact, there is evidence to suggest that these drugs might exacerbate the condition rather than provide relief or improvement. This places additional emphasis on the need for treatment options specifically tailored to the unique challenges of FTD.

The focus of existing treatment strategies for FTD is often on symptom management, with the goal of lessening their intensity. These treatments seek to make daily life more manageable for both the patients and those around them. Additionally, therapeutic interventions may be recommended to address behavioral changes and communication challenges, which are common symptoms that can profoundly affect personal relationships and social interactions.

Non-pharmaceutical approaches are also commonly employed, such as various forms of therapy and lifestyle adjustments, designed to assist individuals in maintaining as much independence and quality of life as possible. Although treating FTD can be complicated, these management techniques can significantly mitigate the impact of symptoms on a patient's daily functioning and interactions with others.

When considering the future prospects for someone with one of the forms of FTD (frontotemporal dementia), it is essential to approach the situation with a sense of realism. The trajectory of FTD is one of progressive decline, affecting various aspects of the individual's abilities. Over time, those with the condition will face significant challenges as their social skills, cognitive abilities including problem-solving and memory, and even neurological functions like movement and coordination continously deteriorate.

The complex nature of FTD's symptoms means that individuals require comprehensive and continuous care, which often leads to the necessity for long-term nursing-home services. Such facilities are equipped to provide the dedicated care and support that can manage the unique needs of dementia patients, ensuring their comfort and safety as the disease advances.

It is vital for families and caregivers to understand that the duration of care needed can vary widely among those living with FTD. Some affected individuals, particularly those who also suffer from an associated condition such as motor neuron disease, may unfortunately succumb to the illness relatively quickly, with lives drawing to a close within approximately five years following a diagnosis.

On the other hand, there are cases where people successfully live with FTD for much longer, with some patients managing to reach up to a decade post-diagnosis. This variance underscores the unpredictable nature of the disease and the importance of individualized care planning. Due to the degenerative nature of FTD, planning for long-term care as early as possible helps in ensuring the best quality of life for the person affected and can aid families and carers to prepare for the challenges ahead both emotionally and practically. FTD imposes a significant change not only on those directly suffering from the condition but also on the network of people around them, which includes family, friends, and healthcare providers. Having an understanding of the disease's progression and being prepared for the long-term implications is crucial in managing the condition with compassion and providing the best care possible for those impacted by this form of dementia.

Chapter 7

Understanding Dementia with Lewy Bodies

In the United Staes, approximately 100,000 individuals are impacted by a distinctive type of dementia known as Dementia with Lewy bodies (DLB). What sets DLB apart are the particular changes that take place within the brain and the assortment of symptoms that individuals experience as a result. Adele, a vibrant and active woman in her late 60s, began to experience vivid dreams that seemed to spill into her waking hours. Her family noticed changes too - not just memory lapses but periods of confusion interspersed with moments of clarity. They assumed it was age catching up until Adele reported seeing unusual objects in her home.

A visit to the neurologist brought forth a diagnosis that was unfamiliar to many - Dementia with Lewy Bodies (DLB). Unlike Alzheimer's or vascular dementia, DLB presented an amalgamation of cognitive, motor, and psychiatric symptoms making it complex and challenging.

Just like Adele, anyone facing the unexpected blueprint that leads towards DLB needs comprehensive understanding and support. This chapter will guide you through the basics of DLB and offer practical advice on managing its unique facets.

Dementia with Lewy bodies plays a significant role in the lives of many older adults and their families. It affects about 1.4 million people in the United States alone, accounting for up to 20% of all dementia cases. This disease doesn't just cause memory problems; it brings along a whole host of other symptoms that can be equally distressing.

DLB is characterized by a progressive decline in mental abilities accompanied by specific symptoms distinct from other forms of dementia. These include visual hallucinations, fluctuating cognition, Parkinsonism (motor symptoms similar to Parkinson's disease), and REM sleep behavior disorder.

According to a study published in the Journal of Alzheimer's Disease, DLB progresses through several stages, each characterized by worsening cognitive and physical symptoms.

1.In the early stage, individuals may experience subtle memory changes, mood swings, and visual hallucinations. They might also have problems with attention and alertness which can fluctuate from day to day or even throughout the same day.

2.As DLB moves into its middle stages, cognitive symptoms become more apparent. Individuals may struggle with problem-solving tasks or complex mental activities. Physically, they may exhibit Parkinsonian symptoms such as rigid muscles, slowed movement or tremors.

3.In late-stage DLB, individuals often require extensive help with daily activities due to significant declines in mental abilities. They may have difficulty recognizing family members and friends. Physical symptoms often worsen leading to increased risk of falls and other injuries.

Understanding these stages is crucial for managing expectations about disease progression and planning care strategies accordingly. The study emphasizes that while there is now no cure for DLB, treatments can temporarily improve symptoms or slow down their progression.

Therefore it's important for those diagnosed with DLB and their caregivers to seek advice from medical professionals who specialize in this field so they can make informed decisions about treatment options based on individual circumstances. But here's something fascinating about DLB; despite its destructive nature, it often leaves pockets of cognitive abilities untouched for longer periods compared to other forms of dementia. It's as if amidst all the chaos and destruction, there are still islands of calm and clarity.

Fluctuations in cognition can make day-to-day life unpredictable. On some days your loved one may appear normal; other days may be marked by confusion or lethargy. Flexibility becomes key when dealing with these shifts.

Addressing Parkinsonism Symptoms

Motor symptoms such as stiffness, slowed movement, and tremors can add to the challenges of DLB. Regular physiotherapy and exercises tailored for Parkinson's patients can help manage these symptoms. Moreover, creating a safe environment to prevent falls becomes essential. Removing tripping hazards and installing grab bars in necessary areas can go a long way in ensuring safety.

Managing REM Sleep Behavior Disorder

REM sleep behavior disorder involves acting out vivid dreams, often leading to disturbed sleep or potential injury. Consult your doctor about potential solutions such as medication adjustments or protective measures around the bed.

Navigating DLB needs understanding its unique facets, adapting to fluctuating cognitive states, addressing motor symptoms, and managing sleep disturbances. Remember that every journey with DLB is unique - what works for one person may not work for another. Patience, flexibility, and a strong support system will be invaluable assets on this journey. But here's the silver lining - understanding these symptoms can help us manage DLB more effectively. Accurate diagnosis allows for targeted treatments, which can significantly improve quality of life. Even simple strategies, like setting up a regular sleep schedule or creating a safe environment for someone experiencing hallucinations, can make a world of difference.

Dementia with Lewy bodies is not just another form of dementia; it's a complex condition that affects every aspect of a person's life. But with understanding comes hope - the hope for better treatments, better care, and ultimately, a better life for those living with DLB.

By implementing the practical advice outlined in this chapter and collaborating closely with healthcare professionals, you can confirm your loved one receives the best care possible while living with DLB. Like Adele's family, you too are now equipped to handle this complex challenge. I met Mary on a sunny Tuesday morning. She was seated by the window, her face turned towards the warm sunlight that streamed through the glass. Her hair was white as snow, and she had a gentle smile on her lips.

Mary was a resident at Rosewood, an assisted living facility. When I first met her, she was diagnosed with dementia with Lewy bodies (DLB). The diagnosis had come after several months of uncertainty when Mary's symptoms didn't fit into any specific category of cognitive disorders. Initially, Mary would have good days and bad days. On good days, she would remember everyone around her - staff members, other residents and even their stories. But on bad days, it seemed like she was lost in a foggy maze. There were times when she couldn't recognize herself in the mirror or recall what day it was.

What set DLB apart from other forms of dementia were two distinct features - vivid hallucinations and fluctuations in cognitive abilities. For Mary, these hallucinations often took the form of small children playing around her room or birds flying indoors. Over time, we noticed another symptom that further confirmed our diagnosis – REM sleep behavior disorder. It meant that Mary physically acted out her dreams during sleep which sometimes led to minor injuries.

To manage these symptoms, Mary relied not just on medication but also non-pharmacological interventions such as maintaining regular routines for meals and bedtime; keeping familiar objects around to provide comfort; using nightlights to reduce disorientation at night; among others. However, there were challenging moments too - like when Mary became anxious because of visual hallucinations or when she couldn't understand why she couldn't join the children who played only in her imagination.

But amidst all this uncertainty and hardship there were beautiful moments too - like when Mary sang old songs word-for-word or remembered past events with crystal clear clarity. Those were the moments that reminded us of the person Mary used to be - a loving mother, a devoted wife, and an avid birdwatcher.

The Uniqueness of Dementia with Lewy Bodies

Though there are various forms of dementia, DLB stands out for specific reasons. To comprehend its uniqueness, we must first look at the defining feature of this disease.

The Discovery of Lewy Bodies

In the early 20th century, Frederick Lewy, a distinguished neurologist, conducted research on the brains of patients who had dementia. In 1912, he observed peculiar spherical protein accumulations within the midbrain and cortex. These aggregated proteins, later named 'Lewy bodies' in his honor, are a hallmark of DLB.

Link to Movement Disorders

Interestingly, Lewy bodies are not exclusive to DLB; they are also present in the brain tissue of individuals suffering from Parkinson's disease. Consequently, those with DLB often show symptoms that are characteristic of movement disorders such as Parkinson's.

The Symptomatology of DLB

Understanding the symptoms of DLB is crucial for diagnosis and support. While DLB shares some commonalities with other dementias, it also has characteristics similar to Parkinson's disease. Diagnosis relies on the identification of two of the three primary symptoms, alongside various secondary symptoms which may also be present.

Core Symptoms

Health professionals look for these prominent symptoms when diagnosing DLB:

1. **Fluctuating Consciousness**

- This is perhaps one of the most confounding aspects of DLB. Individuals may face drastic fluctuations in alertness and cognitive ability. During certain moments or days, a person might exhibit extreme confusion, finding it challenging to perform basic tasks or engage in conversation. Then, unexpectedly, clarity can return allowing them to partake in more complex activities like enjoying movies or playing card games. These swings in consciousness can occur over minutes, hours, or days.

2. **Visual Hallucinations**

- A significant proportion of those with DLB encounter visual hallucinations. These hallucinations are not mere figments of imagination; they are vivid and convincing, making them appear real. While some people might find these hallucinations benign or even entertaining, others can be severely disturbed by frightening visions.

3. **Spontaneous Parkinsonism**

- Mirroring the symptoms of Parkinson's disease, spontaneous Parkinsonism can lead to muscle rigidity, slow and impaired movement, tremors, a noticeable shake, and a diminished expression in the face. These symptoms are often a key indicator of DLB.

Supporting Symptoms

In addition to the core symptoms, individuals with DLB might also experience a range of secondary symptoms:

- Sudden fainting spells
- Frequent falls, which are sometimes unpredictable and can lead to serious injuries
- Difficulty swallowing, which can affect nutrition and increase the risk of choking
- Issues controlling bladder function, known as urinary incontinence
- Delusions, which involve firmly held false beliefs that are not supported by evidence
- Depression, leading to a significant decline in mood and interest in activities once enjoyed
- Physical engagement while dreaming, often in a distressing or violent manner due to REM sleep

disorder, a condition where individuals act out their dreams

Understanding DLB is crucial for patients, families, and caregivers to provide appropriate care and manage symptoms effectively. Recognizing the symptoms early on is essential for developing a treatment and support plan that can greatly enhance the quality of life for those living with DLB. Furthermore, comprehending the full spectrum of the disease's impact on movement, cognition, and emotional well-being can help in navigating the challenges that come with this condition. Encouraging ongoing education about DLB and advocating for research into more effective treatments is fundamental. Through compassionate care, support, and a deeper insight into this complex form of dementia, we can improve the lives of those affected by Dementia with Lewy Bodies.

Understanding the Underlying Factors

The mystery of what leads to Dementia with Lewy Bodies (DLB) lingers, as scientists and medical professionals have yet to pinpoint its exact causes. Family history doesn't appear to be a significant factor, as it seems to occur sporadically rather than being passed down through genetics. Also, extensive research has yet to reveal any genetic mutations or irregularities that consistently contribute to the development of DLB.

Navigating the Diagnostic Process

The diagnosis of DLB is a complex process that relies heavily on a detailed medical history and the clear presence of memory-related decline alongside a specific set of primary and supporting symptoms. At present, there's no definitive scan or test to confirm DLB; brain imaging and other scans are mainly utilized to eliminate other possible causes of dementia such as Alzheimer's disease or vascular dementia. For this reason, healthcare providers place significant weight on the symptomatology and clinical history when making a DLB diagnosis.

Exploring the Current Treatment Landscape

Currently, the medical world is still in search of a cure or specialized treatment specifically for DLB. However, some treatments approved for Alzheimer's disease, like rivastigmine, may offer temporary relief by reducing symptoms and delaying their progression. Rivastigmine, in particular, is noted for its ability to alleviate hallucinations often experienced by those with DLB.

In addition to this, medical experts may prescribe medications to manage various symptoms associated with DLB. For example, Clonazepam is often recommended for the treatment of REM sleep behavior disorder, a common condition in DLB patients where they physically act out vivid and often unpleasant dreams. In dealing with the depression that frequently accompanies DLB, Selective Serotonin Reuptake Inhibitors (SSRIs) such as Prozac may be prescribed to provide some alleviation. It is essential to exercise caution when treating the psychotic symptoms like delusions and hallucinations that individuals with DLB may experience.

Chapter 8:

Understanding Creutzfeldt-Jacobs Disease

I met Sarah during one of my visits to the community center. A lively woman in her early sixties, she was full of life and laughter. Her eyes sparkled with a zest for life that was infectious. We became fast friends, often spending our afternoons playing chess or discussing books.

One day, I noticed something different about Sarah. She seemed distant, her once sparkling eyes now held a vacant look. Our chess games became more infrequent as she would often forget the rules or lose track of the game halfway through.

Sarah's condition worsened over time; it wasn't just memory loss anymore. She began experiencing mood swings, periods of confusion and even difficulty walking. It was heartbreaking to see such a vibrant personality being eroded away by an unseen storm within her mind.

Eventually, Sarah was diagnosed with Creutzfeldt-Jakob Disease (CJD), a rare form of dementia that affects only one in every million people each year worldwide.

CJD is unlike other forms of dementia; it progresses rapidly, often leading to severe disability and death within a year or two after symptoms begin appearing. There is now no cure for CJD which makes its diagnosis all the more devastating.

While Sarah's story may seem bleak, it serves as an important lesson on understanding and recognizing the signs of CJD early on. Early detection doesn't promise a cure, but it can help manage symptoms better and provide patients like Sarah with care that improves their quality of life during their remaining days.

The first signs are usually subtle - memory problems perhaps not severe enough to be classified as dementia yet but noticeable nonetheless if you're paying attention. As these cognitive issues intensify, neurological symptoms such as impaired coordination and visual disturbances start appearing.

According to scientific studies, CJD progresses through several stages, each with its own set of symptoms:

1. Early Stage: The initial symptoms can be subtle and may include memory problems, behavioral changes, poor coordination, and visual disturbances. This stage can last for weeks or months.

2. Middle Stage: As the disease progresses, mental deterioration becomes severe. People may develop involuntary muscle jerks called myoclonus, they may go blind and they often become mute.

3. Late Stage: In the final stage of the disease, persons lose the ability to move or speak and need full-time care.

4. End Stage: This usually involves severe mental impairment (dementia) and loss of physical control. Most

patients die within a year after symptoms appear due to complications such as pneumonia or other infections.

Research is ongoing into potential treatments for CJD - recent studies have looked at using antibodies to stop the spread of abnormal proteins in the brain which cause CJD but these are still in early stages of development.

Sarah's case taught me that while we cannot stop diseases like CJD from taking hold once they've started progressing, we can learn about them, so we're better equipped to deal with their consequences. Understanding CJD and its symptoms can make a world of difference in managing the disease and providing patients with the care they need.

Sarah's story is a stark reminder that life is unpredictable. But it also shows us how knowledge about conditions like CJD can empower us to navigate these unforeseen storms with grace and courage.

Just as a detective meticulously pieces together clues to solve a complex mystery, scientists and researchers are tirelessly working to unravel the enigmatic nature of Creutzfeldt-Jakob Disease (CJD). This rare and devastating form of dementia often leaves families feeling overwhelmed and lost, much like a detective faced with a case full of dead ends.

One of the first ways CJD plays a significant role in daily life is how it affects the brain. This disease, caused by misfolded proteins called prions, leads to rapid neurodegeneration. For example, you may notice that your loved one begins to forget familiar faces or even their own name. These are not mere lapses of memory - they're signs of a relentless disease at work.

Secondly, CJD drastically changes the life of the affected person and their caregivers. The progressive nature of the disease requires constant attention and care, similar to how a newborn baby needs round-the-clock supervision. This is a testament to how life-altering this disease can be, not just for the patient, but for everyone involved.

Thirdly, CJD has profound implications in the medical world. It's one of the few diseases that stay largely untreatable, making it a critical area of research. For instance, studies have shown that prion diseases like CJD could potentially shed light on other neurodegenerative conditions such as Alzheimer's and Parkinson's. This underlines the importance of understanding and studying CJD.

Despite its rarity and complexity, CJD is more than a mere medical term. It's a life-changing reality for many families around the world. Understanding it is like navigating an intricate maze - each turn reveals new challenges and discoveries.

As we continue to delve deeper into this topic, remember that knowledge is power. Understanding Creutzfeldt-Jakob Disease is not just about learning medical jargon. It's about gaining the tools to face this formidable opponent head-on, to provide the best possible care for your loved one, and to contribute to the collective effort to one day solve this complex mystery.

Symptoms

A scientific study published in The Lancet Neurology suggests that CJD often begins subtly with memory problems, behavioral changes, lack of coordination and visual disturbances. As the illness progresses, mental deterioration becomes pronounced with involuntary movements, blindness or weakness of extremities.

Emotionally, patients might feel frustrated because of increasing difficulty performing routine tasks which were once easy for them. Anxiety can also arise from uncertainty about what's happening to them physically and cognitively.

Patients may exhibit depression or apathy long before other symptoms appear. They might experience insomnia or changes in their sleep-wake cycle as well as uncharacteristic behaviors such as aggression or withdrawal from social activities.

In terms of cognitive abilities, patients may experience confusion or disorientation much earlier than those suffering from Alzheimer's disease. This rapid cognitive decline is another distinguishing factor for CJD.

Individuals might exhibit depression or unusual behaviors like agitation or aggression - these are however common in many forms of dementia but tend to occur more rapidly in CJD.

Cognitive memory problems are common early on; however, they tend to be overshadowed by more noticeable physical symptoms like muscle stiffness or twitching.

The physical symptoms include difficulty speaking or swallowing and sudden jerky movements. These symptoms can set CJD apart from other forms of dementia which may not present such physical manifestations.

What sets Creutzfeldt-Jakob Disease apart from other types of dementia is its speed. Most dementias progress slowly over several years; however, typical onset of CJD occurs around age 60 and about 70 percent of individuals die within one year.

To conclude: If you notice rapid neurological decline in yourself or a loved one accompanied by some specific physical symptoms like sudden jerky movements or difficulty speaking/swallowing it could be indicative of something more serious like Creutzfeldt-Jakob Disease. It's important to seek medical advice promptly as early detection can help manage the progression better even though there is currently no cure for this disease.

Diagnosis

It's important to note that CJD is a complex disease, and its diagnosis can be challenging. Therefore, if you or a loved one are experiencing any of these symptoms, it's crucial to seek medical advice from a healthcare professional who specializes in neurology. They will be able to guide you through the necessary tests and evaluations needed for an accurate diagnosis.

A scientific study published in the Journal of Neurology highlights the use of several diagnostic tools to recognize Creutzfeldt-Jacob's disease. These include electroencephalography (EEG), magnetic resonance imaging (MRI), cerebrospinal fluid analysis for 14-3-3 proteins, and most definitively - a brain biopsy.

The EEG often shows characteristic patterns in CJD patients. However, these patterns are not always present and may vary from patient to patient. An MRI can reveal high signal intensities in certain regions of the brain which is typical for CJD but again it's not definitive.

The presence of 14-3-3 proteins in cerebrospinal fluid has been associated with CJD. However, this test alone cannot confirm the diagnosis as these proteins can also be detected in other neurological disorders.

Finally, a brain biopsy remains the gold standard for diagnosing CJD definitively but because of its invasive nature it's rarely performed unless absolutely necessary.

Chapter 9:

Understanding the Risk Factors and Causes

In this chapter, we are going to learn:

- A quick guide to how your brain functions
- Insight into how dementia can impact brain health
- The role of genetics and family history in dementia
- Lifestyle choices that could lower the risk of dementia

We often hear that prevention is better than scrambling for a cure. This rings especially true for conditions like dementia, where the effects are heartbreaking and no cure is yet available. Unfortunately, fending off dementia isn't straightforward. It's not the same as saying, "Wash your hands to prevent a cold," or "Cut down on junk food to avoid weight gain." When it comes to pinpointing exactly what triggers dementia, doctors haven't found a single source. The disease shows up in various forms, which complicates matters. But here's a silver lining: some studies suggest that certain changes in diet and lifestyle, things like staying active both mentally and physically, could help keep dementia at bay.

In this chapter, we're going to explore the different factors that play into the risk of developing dementia. We'll cover everything from genetics to the impact of environmental toxins, and the connection between your level of activity and smoking habits. Before we dig into that, we'll kick things off with a basic explanation of how your brain and memory should function without the interference of disease. Understanding this can give you a leg up in recognizing the signs of dementia and what you might be able to do about preventing it.

Here's something pretty amazing—almost everyone, from little kids with their crayon-stained fingers to our wise grandparents, carries around a little electronic buddy. We have smartphones that can answer any question we toss at them, tablets that store our favorite books, laptops that connect us with friends across oceans, and gaming consoles that can transport us to different worlds—all powered by tiny chips that seem to have minds of their own. It makes you wonder if these gadgets will one day start thinking on their own. But if you take a moment and think about our own 'thinking caps'—our brains—it's kind of wild that there aren't any flashy buttons or cool wires inside. Instead, it just looks like a lumpy, wrinkly blob. When you compare that to other parts of the body, it can be pretty puzzling. I mean, it's easy to see that the heart is working like a pump, your intestines look like twisty slides that food whooshes down, and your lungs are like tiny bubbles filling up with air for breathing. Don't be fooled by its plain looks, though. That waxy-looking thing inside your head is actually super smart.

Just now, my brain is doing this little dance where it tells my hands to tap on the keyboard and makes sure my eyes are tracking the words that pop up on the screen. Meanwhile, it's soaking in some tunes from my iPod and even knows that somewhere behind me, my pet parakeet, is having a grand old time fluttering about. While juggling all that, it's also planning the next sentences I'm going to type, keeping me sitting upright without tipping over, and handling all the stuff that keeps me alive, like breathing and making my heart keep a steady beat—and it's doing it all at the same time, without even breaking a sweat. Yeah, the inside of our heads might not look like much, but it's bustling with activity and cleverness that never takes a break—not even for a minute.

Alright, imagine we're taking a casual deep-dive into one of the most incredible things about us humans – our brain. It might seem like a stretch to cram the universe of brainy knowledge into a single book section, but I'm going to give you the lowdown as best as I can. The brain's like the control center for, well, everything you do. Making sense of complex emotions like love or cranking out those sweet dance moves – it takes some serious brainpower. And even though figuring it all out is pretty tough, we've got to start somewhere, right?

Getting to Know Your Brain

Think of the brain as this squishy, wrinkly command station that weighs about three pounds (kind of like a heavy loaf of whole-grain bread) and feels like that soft tofu you find at the grocery store. Inside this amazing organ, you've got around 86 billion neurons – these are tiny but mighty cells that chat with each other and make all the magic happen. The brain is split into two parts called hemispheres. Imagine it like a walnut, with two halves that look almost the same but do different things. Each side is chopped up further into sections known as lobes - there are four of them with fancy names: frontal, parietal, temporal, and occipital. Now, picture the brain like a very smart mushroom sitting on top of a stalk (that's your spinal cord), and it has this little backpack attached called the cerebellum. All of these parts work together to help you live, learn, and experience the world in your own unique way. There you go! A friendly peek into the mind-blowing world of the brain. Trust me, there's so much more to discover, and each bit plays a part in making you who you are.

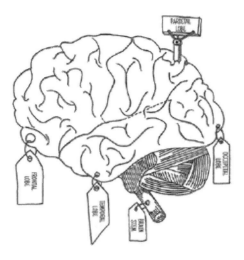

Take a peek at Figure 1, where you'll see a picture of the human brain.

Now, imagine the brain is filled with tiny messengers racing around. These messengers are called neurons, and they're sort of like the electrical wires in your house, but for your brain. They zip electrical signals from one area of the brain to another so different parts can chat with each other.

When observing the nerves in the brain, it becomes evident that they function similarly to roads used by messengers to relay messages. Intriguingly, these signals necessitate jumping across minuscule gaps known as synapses. At these junctures, a neuron dispatches a chemical signal to another, likened to tossing a ball that bears a message. The receiving neuron employs receptors to catch this, thereby initiating an electric signal that forwards the message onward. This process resembles an intricate game of telephone, illustrating the complex and fascinating way in which this tag game operates. In this whole process, there are special chemicals known as neurotransmitters, and some of them, like dopamine, glutamate, and acetylcholine, are super important when we talk about dementia. They play a huge role in how messages are sent and received, and understanding them can help us learn more about this condition.

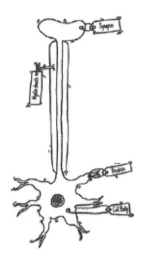

Figure 2: The Nerve Cell

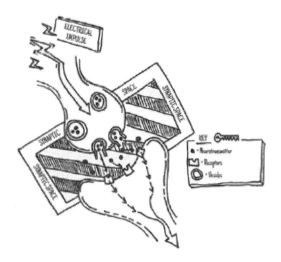

Figure 3: A synapse

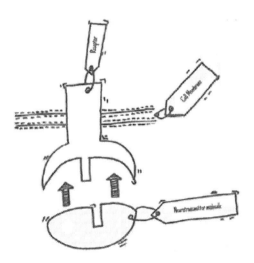

Figure 4 illustrates a transmitter 'connecting' with a receptor.

To really understand what goes off track in our brains when dementia strikes, it's super helpful to know what each part of the brain does. Here's a simple guide to the brain's parts and their jobs:

- **Cerebral hemispheres**: These are the big, main parts of your brain, split by a deep groove. The outer layer is called the cortex and is that gray stuff you hear about – the "gray matter."
- **Frontal lobe**: Right up front in the brain, this section is a real powerhouse, especially for us humans. It's where we do our complex thinking, like making plans or solving problems. It's because of the frontal lobe that we've come so far, from shaping our world to exploring space! This lobe is also where our emotions, speech, and movements are managed.
- **Parietal lobe**: This part is your body's command center for moving around. It's also where your sensations get processed, so basically, it helps you understand what you're touching, feeling, or whether you're standing up straight or tilted.
- **Temporal lobe**: Dementia often hits this area hard. It's home to the hippocampus, which is all about memory, and that's why memory loss is a big deal with dementia. The temporal lobe also handles hearing and understanding what people are saying to you.
- **Occipital lobe**: This is your visual processing center – dealing with sights, shapes, and colors.
- **Brain stem**: Think of this as the brain's old-school core that keeps you ticking without you having to think about it – it handles basic life stuff like breathing and keeping your heart beating. Damage here is usually serious business.

- **Cerebellum**: It might look weird, like a cauliflower stuck on the back of the brain, but it's really important. It keeps you balanced, upright, and coordinated. If this part isn't doing its job, probably after a few too many drinks, you'll definitely notice the difference!
- **Cerebrospinal fluid (CSF)**: This fluid wraps around your brain and spinal cord, offering protection and carrying important nutrients.

Understanding these different parts can make the complicated topic of brain function a bit easier to digest, especially when talking about conditions like dementia that affect so many of us and our loved ones. Think of cerebrospinal fluid, or CSF for short, as the body's built-in protective helmet for your brain and spinal cord. This special fluid flows around the brain and spinal cord, and doctors sometimes need to collect a sample of it through a procedure called a lumbar puncture. CSF has two big jobs. Firstly, it's like a clean-up crew that takes away the waste products from the brain cells' activities. And secondly, it acts like a cushion that helps to protect the brain from getting hurt, like if someone hits their head or is in a car crash. Moving onto ventricles, these are kind of like the hallways in your brain that the CSF moves through. They're found in both halves of the brain and can get bigger in some forms of dementia because the brain cells around them can shrink or disappear.

When we talk about the cortex, we're not discussing a specific spot in the brain. Instead, it's like the brain's outer layer or skin. The cortex is super important because it handles a lot of different tasks, depending on which part of the brain it covers. It's involved in how we remember things, how we think, our ability to use language, and even what makes us conscious. Essentially, the cortex has a huge role in all the stuff that makes us uniquely human.

Here's a down-to-earth take on how our memory ticks.

The brain is kind of like a mysterious library where not all the books have been read yet, even with all the fancy research tools we've got today. But getting the gist of the simple stuff, especially when it comes to memory, can shine a light on what goes haywire when folks face diseases like dementia.

Memory is super important for everyday life. When it starts to crumble, it really throws a wrench in the works. Imagine not being able to learn from yesterday, or make any plans for tomorrow. You'd be all kinds of lost—not just in finding your way around town but also lost in your feelings, struggling to keep up with chores, or zoning out halfway through a chat. If your memory isn't on point, you'll stumble following instructions and even blank out on faces of those you cherish.

We humans have two main memory zones: the short-term and the long-term.

Short-term Memory

This one's like a sticky note for your brain. It holds onto things like phone numbers or what your friend just asked you to grab from the shop. But it's a small sticky note that clears off pretty fast to make room for new info. We can usually hold onto about seven to nine things for half a minute before they start to vanish. Unless, of course, we keep repeating the info like a mantra. If we want to remember something for longer, we've got to move it over into the long-term memory vault, where there's heaps of room, and things can stick around for ages.

Long-term Memory

Now, this is where all the good stuff gets stored for the long haul. Think of your first address, your favorite teacher's name, or even sports scores from decades ago. And it's not just facts—the long-term memory saves the how-to's of life as well, like riding a bike, lacing up shoes, or driving.

These memories aren't just dumped in one brain spot; they're actually a team effort across different parts.

And there's more—long-term memory has a couple of different cupboards:

- Declarative memory: This is where all your experiences, your know-how on the meaning of words, and things like phone numbers and facts go.
- Procedural memory: Think of this as the memory toolbox for actions—everything from steering your bike to tying your shoelaces.

How Memory Works Its Magic

For memory to do its thing, three steps need to happen smoothly:

1. Encoding (where your brain picks up and tags info)
2. Storage (keeping it safe in your brain)
3. Retrieval (pulling the info back out when you need it)

Any stumbles in these steps, and memory can go awry. You might encode and save the information just fine, but if you can't pull it back out, it's as if it's not there. Or maybe you encode something, but it never really gets saved—then, of course, you won't be able to find it later. Memory's a bit finicky but understanding these basics can help us sympathize with those when memory's not all there and remind us to treasure our own recollections and keep our brains in tip-top shape.

Dementia really messes with the brain and its ability to carry out its usual tasks. Essentially, it boils down to issues with the brain cells—either they can't chat with each other because they're not getting enough oxygen, which is what happens in vascular dementia, or weird protein chunks start clogging up the works. These junky bits are called plaques and tangles in Alzheimer's disease and are known as Lewy bodies in Lewy body dementia.

I know that might sound way too basic, but it helps us get the gist of how a single, or usually a whole bunch, of brain cells can start to drop the ball. When the brain cells flunk, and there's not enough of the chemical messengers that help them communicate, it's like parts of the person's central nervous system just start to shut down.

It's not just about the type of damage; it's also where it happens in the brain that affects the symptoms of dementia. Each kind of dementia brings its own set of issues:

- With Fronto-temporal dementia, it's mostly the front parts of the brain that get hit—the parts that handle complex thoughts and memories. This leads to symptoms like trouble with planning and drastic personality shifts.

- Alzheimer's disease goes after the hippocampus, a bit of the brain crucial for making memories last. That's why people often first notice that they can't remember recent things, but older memories can still come through.
- Lewy body disease spreads damage throughout the cortex, messing with both how we move and our senses. It often causes hallucinations and movement problems.
- Vascular dementia is a bit of a wildcard. Since it links to blood flow issues which can pop up anywhere, the symptoms vary a lot. Memory, personality, even physical movements can all take a hit depending on which brain part is affected.

Look, the brain is super complex, and dementia symptoms are tricky—they don't stick to neat borders and can affect many brain parts, particularly with memory. Plus, when the pathways connecting different brain areas get damaged, that brings a whole other set of difficulties. In this chapter, we're trying to shine a light on the often-overlooked realities of dementia with a mix of empathy and insightful information. Because understanding the challenge is the first step toward compassionate care. Getting older definitely has its challenges—just ask anyone who's been through it. If I had a dollar for each time someone told me "growing old is no walk in the park," I might be lounging on a tropical beach instead of here. Though, honestly? No one actually pays me to say that. I do hear it quite often, and it rings true. Aging is tough on the body. Eyesight gets blurry, joints ache and complain no matter what you do, and hearing starts to fade. Many men start losing their hair, too. Then there's the drop in energy, sex drive, and sometimes even the quickness of your mind. But, and this might surprise some, getting older doesn't automatically mean you'll get dementia.

On the other hand, dementia isn't just something that only impacts older people. Though it's more common as we get older, younger folks can experience it as well. The Alzheimer's Society points out that while about 1 in 14 people over 65 could develop dementia, there are also around 17,000 people under 65 with dementia in the United States alone. And since only 44% of those with dementia have been diagnosed in England, Wales, and Northern Ireland, the number might jump up as more people learn about their condition. When it comes to different types of dementia, the reasons vary, especially with age. Younger people could have Alzheimer's, vascular dementia, Lewy body disease, or fronto-temporal dementia. But after 75, most dementia diagnoses are Alzheimer's, with a few other types mixed in. It's like a funnel—wide at the beginning with many possibilities and narrowing down as you get older to mostly one kind. Learning all this might be tough, but understanding what's happening can help us face these challenges with kindness and find the support that we or our loved ones need.

Know the roles of Family history and Genetics

Sometimes our health can be linked to our family tree because certain medical issues tend to show up in families across generations. It's not about catching something from someone else or picking up a bad habit; it's just part of our DNA — the stuff that makes us who we are. For example, color-blindness often runs in families, and so does Huntington's disease, although it's a lot less common. Then there are health problems that don't show up automatically but may appear if the conditions are set — think of it as a possibility tucked away in our genes. Someone might have a higher chance of facing mental health challenges like schizophrenia, especially if they go through really tough times in their life.

Remember, this doesn't mean having a family history of a condition guarantees you'll have it too. It's just that the odds might be a little different compared to someone without that family history. It's essential to understand this connection between our genes and our health, but also to know that it's not the whole story. Life's ups and downs play a big role too. Imagine each person as a unique Lego set that comes with 20,000 to 25,000 instruction pieces, and those pieces are what we call genes. They're tucked away safely in every single cell of our body, and they hold the secrets to all sorts of things that make you, well, you!

From your hair color to the size of your feet, the genes are in charge. They even decide how tall you grow and what your voice sounds like. And yes, they're the ones that determine whether you're a guy or a gal too. All these genes are neatly packed on something called chromosomes – think of these as neat little storage boxes. You've got 23 pairs of them, and you get half from your mom and the other half from your dad, so it's a family affair!

Now, these genes and chromosomes are made from a super special chemical called deoxyribonucleic acid. But that's a mouthful, so just say DNA, and everyone will know what you mean. DNA is made up of four building blocks, kind of like the alphabet of your body's blueprint. These are:

- Adenine (A)
- Cytosine (C)
- Guanine (G)
- Thymine (T)

The DNA strands are like sentences made up of this four-letter alphabet, and just like in any language, the order of these 'letters' matters a lot. They spell out the instructions for all the things that make up who you are. For instance, a DNA 'sentence' like AGTACCCTTACGACT might tell your body one thing about your traits, while CCCGTTATATGCTA might say something completely different. Think of it all as an incredibly intricate recipe book that's been passed down through generations, telling your body how to put everything together. It's a complex process for sure! Just to give you a visual, there's a way these DNA strands curl and twist to form the genes, and they bundle up to become the chromosomes we talked about.

I hope this gives you a better glimpse into the fantastic world of genetics. It's a bit like getting a peek behind the curtain to see how the magic happens in your very own body!

Imagine a perfect world where our DNA is the blueprint for nothing but good health, blockbuster movie-star looks, and a life that never ends. That would be something, wouldn't it? But the reality is a bit different. Illness is a part of life, when most of us look in the mirror, we don't quite see the reflection of Angelina Jolie or Brad Pitt smiling back, and the truth is, everyone's time comes to an end eventually, for some earlier than others. Interestingly, it's these genetic quirks and changes over time that have actually helped humans get ahead, giving some of us a leg up in strength, smarts, or looks. It's not all sunshine and roses though, because the same changes that can give us advantages can also pass on diseases to the next generation.

Here's a little nugget of hope, though – since you get half your genes from one parent and the other half from your second parent, this mix-up means there's a chance for less helpful genes to get weeded out over time. Still, some families find certain health issues popping up generation after generation. Remember, understanding our genetic cookbook is a big step toward better health and compassion for each other. It's fascinating and a little complex, but definitely worth knowing about. It's pretty common to get sucked into wild stories about how everything around us is risky. If you paid attention to every scary headline about pollutants or what's in our food and makeup, you'd never want to go outside. But what's really true? Especially when it comes to something serious like dementia, do things we come across every day actually play a role? It's a big question.

I've really dug deep online and into scientific articles to see if I'm missing something. But, as far as I can see, although it's a good idea to be mindful about what you eat and the air you breathe, there's no solid proof that points to our environment as a cause for dementia. Sure, some studies suggest that dirty air might affect the thinking abilities of older folks, yet there's no hard proof that it could lead to dementia.

The Well-known Aluminium Debate

Back in 1965, a group of researchers did something pretty harsh. They injected aluminium into rabbits' brains and later on, those rabbits showed signs similar to what doctors see in people with Alzheimer's disease brains. That experiment kickstarted the whole fear that aluminium, which is pretty much everywhere, could be linked to dementia. There have been all sorts of scares over the years, like worries about using aluminium pots or antiperspirants. Despite a ton of research since then, no one's managed to prove there's a connection. For now, everyone agrees aluminium is generally safe, just as long as you're not literally putting it into your brain

Staying Healthy: Down-to-Earth Tips for Prevention

When it comes to living healthily, no one's perfect. I like to stay active by running marathons and cycling long distances, but I'm the first to admit that I enjoy a good pastry and a soda every now and then.

We all know what we *should* be doing when it comes to health – heck, every doctor's visit and public health ad reminds us. The basics are plastered everywhere:

- Avoid drugs
- Cut down on the booze
- Quit smoking
- Eat more fruits and veggies
- Skip the fast food
- Get some exercise

Booze and Drugs

Honestly, illegal drugs just aren't worth it. I've seen their havoc firsthand, and while they might not cause dementia directly, they sure don't do your thinking any favors.

Drinking's another one that's got its downsides. There's even a dementia, Korsakoff's syndrome, linked to alcohol. If you're overdoing it, having a talk with your doctor can really make a difference. Over boozing doesn't just threaten your memory but wreaks havoc on just about every organ.

Smoking - Just No

I wish I could make it clearer, but simply put: don't smoke. It's the arch-enemy of living long and well, and it even doubles your risk of dementia by attacking your brain cells and blood vessels. There are loads of quit aids out there—from nicotine gum to e-cigarettes to support groups—all through your healthcare provider.

If you're worried about dementia and there's no family trend, stubbing out the smokes is a much bigger deal than ditching your metal cookware.

Eat Smart

People with a lot of extra weight are more likely to develop dementia. Eating lots of fatty foods increases your risk, too, by damaging blood vessels and reducing blood flow to the brain.

Go for a diet that's low in fat and high in fiber. The golden rule? Five daily servings of fruits and vegetables. They prevent your arteries from clogging and contain antioxidants that defend your brain. Guys should stick to less than 30 grams of saturated fat per day, and gals less than 20. Cut back on the heavy meat, pies, full-fat dairy, and snacks like crisps and cookies. Fill up on wholegrain bread, brown rice, beans, peas, lentils, nuts, and bran-rich cereals instead. Aim for 18 grams of fiber daily to keep your diet on track.

Staying healthy doesn't have to be a chore or about perfection. Small, manageable changes can make a big difference in your life, not just now, but for your future self as well. Be kind to your body – it's the only place you've got to live.

Exercise Made Simple

Moving your body isn't just good for your heart; it's also a bulletproof vest for your brain health, guarding against Alzheimer's and other memory-related problems. Here's the good news – you don't need to become a gym fanatic or run marathons (unless that's your thing). Staying in shape can be as easy as a quick 30-minute walk, five times a week. You don't have to do much. Maybe get off the bus earlier than usual, opt for stairs instead of elevators, or turn dog walks into a daily habit. Love swimming or cycling? Great, and remember, even a small dash of extra effort in day-to-day life goes a long way.

Stay Sharp and Social

Those brain-training apps and games are everywhere, promising a quicker and smarter brain. But hold on – turns out these might not be the mental miracle workers they claim to be. Instead, doing things like learning new skills, exploring new hobbies, or solving crossword puzzles gives your brain a real workout.

And don't forget about hanging out with people. Good conversation and community are like super food for your brain. It could be a party, dance classes, or discussing the latest book club pick – just get mingling!

Risks in Real Life

Life's full of risks; that's just part of the deal. Watching the news, we see how unpredictable things can be. Take the Brazilian soccer fan who tragically passed away from a heart attack during a tension-filled World Cup match. Life is like that – unpredictable.

Even if you're told your risk of dementia is high, that's not set in stone. Staying healthy ups your odds of staying sharp as a tack. And honestly, everyday risks probably pose a more immediate danger than dementia does. Remember the basics: look both ways crossing the street, don't smoke, and buckle up in the car. Stick with these, and chances are you'll stay on the right track.

Chapter 10

Understanding The Stages Of Dementia

Inside This Section:

- Navigating the three main phases of dementia
- Learning how dementia evolves across various conditions

When it comes to dementia, everyone's experience is uniquely their own, yet this condition gradually worsens over time. It's often more straightforward to think of dementia in three broad phases—early, middle, and late—for a clearer picture of the changes that happen as the disease progresses. It's important to remember that these stages aren't rigid. Just like the people they affect, the boundaries between each stage can be fuzzy, and everyone goes through it a bit differently. Factors such as a person's personality before dementia, other health issues they might have, and the level of support they receive have a huge impact on their experience.

Despite these differences, the stages I'll share with you offer a general idea of what you might expect after someone is diagnosed with dementia. We'll kick things off by discussing dementia as a whole, mainly focusing on Alzheimer's disease, which is the most common form. Towards the end, we'll touch on some unique aspects of other types of dementia, such as vascular dementia, fronto-temporal dementia, and Lewy body disease. Remember, understanding dementia is key to providing compassionate care and support to those affected.

When someone starts showing possible signs of dementia, it's really hard to pin down what's happening. That's because the early stage of dementia can be pretty vague. Some people might start forgetting things all of a sudden, or maybe they've been having a little bit of trouble thinking clearly for a while now. The tricky part is that these symptoms can show up in any order and move fast or slow—it really depends on the person. It would be super helpful if illnesses played by the rules and matched what we read about them in books. If that were the case, doctors could quickly figure out what's wrong, start treating it, and the person would have a much better chance of getting better. But that's not how life works—not with being healthy, and certainly not with dementia.

Early on, dementia shows up in different ways for different people. Some might confuse their doctor with symptoms that don't make much sense at first. These unusual signs might even send doctors on a wild goose chase, thinking it could be a ton of other illnesses. Others might walk into their doctor's office with symptoms that practically scream dementia. It's just that clear.

No matter how it appears, early dementia does two big things to a person: it brings change and loss. These aren't just little changes; you might see big shifts in their memory, mood, personality, and how well they can do everyday stuff. They might start losing things a lot, like keys or wallets, but that's not all. You're likely to feel a sense of loss too—like you're missing a part of the relationship you had with them, and they're losing bits of themselves that made them who they are.

Honestly, expecting the unexpected is the best approach with dementia because you can't predict exactly how it will show up 100% of the time.

It's important to pay attention to the early warning signs of dementia, although not everyone will show all of these. Here's what to look out for:

- **Forgetting the Small Stuff**: It's often little things that go first, like names, important dates, or why you walked into a room. If someone starts forgetting these more and more, it might be time to talk to a doctor.
- **Trouble Following Conversations**: If your friend or loved one is getting lost in talks, repeating themselves, or asking the same questions, it could be a sign that something's up.
- **Hard Time with Change**: When everyday changes become overwhelming, or when someone who loved new experiences starts resisting them, these could be clues.

- **Misplacing Things More Often**: Everyone loses their keys or glasses now and then. But if it's happening a lot, or things are showing up in odd places, it's something to note.
- **Decision-Making Gets Tricky**: Watch out if simple choices, like picking a holiday spot or deciding between two shirts, start to feel like big hurdles.
- **Money Confusion**: Keep an eye open if handling money gets confusing or if someone starts falling for sales pitches that don't really make sense for them.
- **Mood Changes**: Feeling down, nervous, uncertain, or grumpy more than usual, or stepping back from friends and hobbies, can also be early dementia signs.

Remember, these changes could happen to anyone. If you notice them in someone you care about, approach the situation with kindness and suggest seeing a doctor for their peace of mind and yours.

Understanding the Journey Through Dementia's Middle Stage

I'm sorry if it seems like I'm going over the same thing again, but honestly, dementia is such a curveball. How long someone can stay in the early phase before hitting that tougher middle stage is anyone's guess. It sure would make life easier for both the person going through it and their caregivers if things were more predictable, with a set timeline to prepare for what's coming next. But dementia doesn't play by those rules – while some folks manage to stay in the early stage for a good stretch of time, others seem to zip right through it, facing harder challenges much sooner.

When Dementia Becomes Undeniable

Once the middle stage kicks in, those once-in-a-while symptoms start to become a constant companion, and things can start changing faster. This stage brings more frequent memory slips, trouble with everyday tasks like cooking, shopping, or getting dressed, and you'll begin to notice bigger shifts in the person's mood and behavior. At this point, it's hard to just brush off these changes as typical 'senior moments' or an expected move into eccentricity as someone gets older. It's clear something more serious is going on, and that's when talking to a doctor to figure out what's happening, and what you can do, isn't just a good idea – it's crucial.

Understanding How Symptoms Progress

When someone's early dementia symptoms get worse, they might:

- **Forget more often:** People might not remember the names of close friends or family, miss important dates, and might even do things that are risky like forgetting a pan on the stove, eating spoiled food, or leaving their house open when they go out.
- **Struggle with talking:** They might repeat themselves a lot or not join in conversations because it's hard to keep up. Finding the right words can be tough, so they might describe objects instead, like calling a watch "the thing that tells time on my wrist." They can also make up stories without meaning, filling in memory gaps with these tales, especially when talking about recent events.
- **Misplace things:** It can be common for them to lose track of where they are, wandering and not being able to find the way back or to where they

intended to go. It's not out of the ordinary for them to get mixed up between day and night, sometimes going outside in their pajamas.

- **Experience mood changes:** There might be more signs of sadness, anger, or mood swings, and sometimes they might act out of character, like making inappropriate comments to people they don't know. They can become very anxious, too, often following loved ones around and looking for comfort from them.
- **Become suspicious:** It's not uncommon for them to feel paranoid, maybe accusing others of stealing or being against them, which can sometimes lead to aggressive behavior.
- **Need help with personal care:** Things like bathing, changing clothes, and dental hygiene might not happen without a reminder. Incontinence might start happening, which makes cleanliness even more of a challenge.

It's really important to approach these changes with patience and understanding. Remember that this is a tough time for them, and they're not acting this way on purpose. Offering gentle reminders and support can make a big difference in their quality of life.

When someone reaches the late stage of dementia, things get pretty tough. At this point, the person could really need a lot of help with day-to-day stuff and might even be living in a care home. Everyone's different, but generally, this signals the beginning of the end.

It's clear now that dementia isn't just about forgetting stuff. It's way more than that. In this last phase, folks lose their ability to live on their own and make sense of the world. There's a deep sense of losing who they are. It's not just the mind that struggles; the body does too. People with advanced dementia often can't do simple tasks anymore. They become weak, have a hard time with balance, and can get very sick very easily.

Sure, not everyone's the same, and you'll find some exceptions. But for most, any strength or skills they had left start to fade. What does this look like? They might need to use a wheelchair and later on, stay in bed. Eating becomes hard, especially if they can't swallow well, and they might lose a lot of weight. Memories slip away to the point where they might not remember what happened that morning or even recognize their family, which is really heartbreaking. Talking can become really hard, too. They might repeat the same words or sounds and not understand when others talk to them, making conversations almost impossible.

People with dementia can also get upset or frustrated easily. Despite all the good intentions, they might not respond well to those trying to help them, which can include yelling or not wanting to cooperate. This can be incredibly tough for family and friends, especially when they're just trying to show their love and care but face rejection.

It's important to talk about these things - not just the facts but the feelings too. Knowing what to expect and understanding the tough emotions involved can hopefully make it a bit easier for everyone who's navigating this challenging time.

Understanding Variations In other types of Dementia

When we think about the changes that dementia brings, a lot of us picture what happens with Alzheimer's. This is the main road that many people with dementia go down. But dementia is a bit like a tree with many branches. Each type has its own quirks and takes a person on a unique path. Here's a friendly guide through this complex terrain.

Vascular Dementia

Imagine a regular path suddenly interrupted by roadblocks; this is often what living with vascular dementia is like. Its root cause is usually a series of strokes or mini-strokes. Each event can alter the landscape of a person's mind, and their abilities can change quickly. Sometimes their talents and memories may seem to wane overnight. However, not every case of vascular dementia fits this pattern because sometimes the problem comes down to the arteries becoming stiff over time. When this happens, changes in the brain sneak up more slowly, mirroring how Alzheimer's unfolds. There's also a glimmer of hope here: if no new strokes occur, the person might not experience worsening symptoms – which is wonderful news indeed. Another striking thing about vascular dementia is that it's more selective – it doesn't cast as wide a net as Alzheimer's. Because strokes hit specific spots, some parts of a person's brain might remain untouched. This can mean that despite some significant struggles, other abilities stay intact, unlike in Alzheimer's where the disease's impact is much broader.

Towards the later stages, though, both Alzheimer's and vascular dementia look pretty similar. Yet people with vascular dementia may hold onto their personality stronger and longer, which sadly means they might be acutely aware of their challenges, leading to a higher risk of feeling blue. Finally, the shadow looming over those with vascular dementia is different. Their heart and blood vessels are the main areas of concern and these complications often lead to their passing, rather than the dementia itself. It's a tough reality, but knowing what to watch out for can arm us with

understanding and prepare us to walk this path with
compassion.

Fronto-Temporal Dementia: What You Need to Know

When we talk about fronto-temporal dementia, we're
looking at a type of dementia that's a bit different from
what most people expect. This one can show up earlier in
life—often when someone is still in their middle years, not
when they're much older. One clear sign that someone
might be dealing with this kind of dementia is a change in
how they interact with others. Here are some things you
might notice:

- They might seem less interested in stuff they used
  to care about (that's called apathy).
- They could act out of line in social settings or with
  their sexual behavior.
- They might start following strict routines or get
  really focused on specific things.

Sometimes, these changes can lead to big life shifts—like
suddenly wanting to change jobs, leave relationships, pick
up new diets, or listen to completely different music.
Another thing about fronto-temporal dementia is that,
especially early on, a person's memory might still be quite
sharp, which isn't always the case with other types of
dementia. But as time goes on, memory issues do start to
crop up.

In the later stages, the challenges get tougher. A person
might:

- Wander around a lot without any clear direction.
- Become apathetic and even stop speaking much.
- Struggle with bladder control.
- Find eating and swallowing hard to do.

These struggles are similar to what folks with Alzheimer's disease might go through. Typically, after someone starts showing symptoms of fronto-temporal dementia, they might live another six to eight years. Understanding this condition can be tough—not just for the person facing it, but also for their loved ones. Knowing what to look out for and what we might expect can help us prepare and offer the best support we can.

Lewy body disease

Lewy body disease starts uniquely because a person's thinking can swing up and down. They might feel clear-headed one moment and confused the next, all within the same day. This is different from the early memory loss seen in Alzheimer's.

In the middle to late stages of Lewy body disease, some common symptoms are:

- Seeing things that aren't there (hallucinations)
- Sudden movement issues like in Parkinson's disease
- Falling down a lot, fainting spells, and even blacking out
- Dreaming out loud (a sleep disorder called REM behavior disorder)
- Trouble swallowing

Unfortunately, as the disease gets worse, people with Lewy body disease need someone to take care of them all the time. They might not be able to leave their beds toward the end. Often, they pass away due to severe lung infections caused by swallowing problems, when food or drink goes into their lungs instead of their stomach. Also, because they fall a lot, they might get hurt or break bones easily. On average, people may live around five to seven years after finding out they have the disease.

When people find out they have a serious illness, they naturally want to know how long they have left. I struggle with this question because predicting life expectancy isn't an exact science. We don't always fit into neat little boxes, and many things can influence how long someone lives. Like Richard Dawkins puts it, humans are like "survival machines" for our genes – we've evolved to be really good at living.

Predicting how long you'll live with a condition like dementia isn't straightforward because of factors like these:

- How advanced the disease was when it got spotted
- Your age when you were diagnosed
- Any other health issues you have
- How well you handle treatments
- Your mental health
- Your immune system's strength
- Your living situation and support network

Everyone reacts differently to diseases like dementia. Having some idea of what might happen can help you plan for the future, which is why people often ask how long they'll live. In general, though, the prognosis for dementia isn't great. A study in 2008 found that on average, women live about 4.6 years after diagnosis, and men about 4.1 years. But these are average numbers. Depending on who you ask, the expected lifespan after finding out you have dementia can range from as short as 3.5 years to as long as

20 years. Usually, the older you are when diagnosed, the shorter the time you might have. Considering that it usually takes about 2.8 years to diagnose from when the disease starts, it's really hard to give a precise number for life expectancy.

Chapter 11

The D.I.C.E. Approach

Dementia is a complex condition characterized by cognitive decline and behavioral changes. One of the most challenging aspects of dementia care is managing these behavioral symptoms which may include agitation, aggression, wandering, depression, apathy and hallucinations.

Scientific studies have shown that the DICE (Describe, Investigate, Create, and Evaluate) approach can be highly effective in managing behavioral issues in dementia patients.

The DICE approach encourages caregivers to understand what triggers certain behaviors in their patients and then develop strategies to prevent or manage them. It promotes individualized care based on each patient's unique needs and circumstances.

DICE is an acronym that stands for Describe, Investigate, Create and Evaluate. It's a method used by healthcare professionals to manage and treat behavioral symptoms in people with dementia.

According to a study published in the Journal of the American Geriatrics Society, DICE has been shown to be effective in reducing behavioral problems associated with dementia without resorting to medication. The approach encourages caregivers and health professionals to work together to understand the reasons behind challenging behaviors and develop strategies for managing them.

The first step, Describe, involves identifying and understanding the behavior that is causing concern. This includes noting when it happens, what triggers it, and how it affects both the person with dementia and their caregiver.

Investigate comes next. This step needs looking at all possible factors contributing to the behavior such as physical discomfort or environmental factors like noise or crowd.

Create is about developing a plan of action tailored specifically for the individual based on information gathered from previous steps.

Finally, Evaluate asks caregivers to assess whether or not their interventions are working over time.

So, if you're caring for someone with dementia who exhibits challenging behaviors, consider trying out the DICE approach. Understand their behavior patterns better by observing closely when they occur and what precedes them. Then create a tailored strategy that addresses these specific triggers or situations.

Remember that patience is key - it might take some time before you see improvement but stick with it because science has shown this method can work wonders!

Chapter 12

Understanding Dementia Treatments

In This Section:

- Learn about medications that aim to ease dementia symptoms.

- Discover how certain drugs can help with emotional wellbeing.
- Be aware of possible side effects from prescription medications.

Medical science has come a long way, offering relief for a myriad of health issues ranging from the common cold to more serious conditions like heart disease. However, not every problem can be solved with a pill, and there are still diseases we're learning how to treat better.

Sadly, dementia falls into this tricky category. Right now, there's no cure-all for the causes of dementia. But the good news is there are some medications out there that can slow down its progression and improve the symptoms for a while. Additionally, other medicines can help handle some of dementia's tough challenges, like sleep problems, hallucinations, and feelings of depression. Everyone experiences dementia differently, so not all medications work for every person. And sometimes, even when doctors prescribe medication with the best intentions, it might not work out well. This could be because the medication has side effects, or it doesn't play well with other medications the person is already taking. With these precautions in mind, we're going to explore the current medications available that bring some relief to those with dementia, while also being real about the limitations these treatments may have. As the disease progresses, your loved you may experience difficulty swallowing. This is known as dysphagia and can lead to malnutrition and dehydration if not addressed promptly. Also, people with dementia often have other chronic conditions like heart disease or diabetes that need ongoing management. It could be a loss of mobility leading to falls or bedsores from prolonged bed rest.

Navigating these challenges needs vigilance and patience. Regular check-ups are essential to watch their overall health status and manage any chronic conditions effectively. Behavioral changes are common in people with dementia. These may include mood swings, agitation, aggression or even hallucinations. As a caregiver, it's important to stay calm and patient during these episodes while seeking professional help when necessary. Behavioral management strategies can significantly improve the quality of life for both patients with dementia and their caregivers.

Patience is key here; remember that your loved one isn't acting out intentionally - it's just part of the disease progression. Infections are more prevalent among those suffering from dementia because of their weakened immune system combined with poor hygiene practices resulting from cognitive impairment.

Good hygiene practices are crucial in preventing infections. A study published in the Journal of Alzheimer's Disease found that pneumonia, urinary tract infections (UTIs), and skin infections were among the most common types of infection in people with dementia. The research also indicated that these individuals had a significantly higher mortality rate from these infections compared to those without dementia.

The researchers concluded that prevention strategies should be a priority when caring for patients with dementia. This includes Regular hand washing, clean living spaces, and proper dental care. Maintaining good personal hygiene, keeping wounds clean and dry, staying up to date on vaccinations, and managing chronic conditions like diabetes which can increase the risk of infection.

In addition to this, proper hydration and nutrition play an essential role in preventing UTIs and skin infections respectively. It is therefore crucial for caregivers to confirm that individuals with dementia consume enough fluids throughout the day and eat balanced meals.

Moreover, it is recommended by experts in geriatric care that routine medical check-ups should not be overlooked as they provide an opportunity for early detection and treatment of potential health issues. While caring for someone with dementia can be challenging due to their unique needs, implementing preventive measures against infection based on scientific evidence can greatly improve their quality of life.

Lastly but importantly is pain management; Pain is a significant issue for people living with dementia. The nature of the disease often makes it difficult for patients to talk about their discomfort, leading to under-recognition and under-treatment of pain. Over half of all dementia patients experience substantial pain. However, because these people may not be able to articulate their suffering due to cognitive impairment, they are often unable to receive appropriate treatment. Untreated or under-treated pain can exacerbate symptoms of dementia such as agitation and confusion. It can also lead to decreased mobility and increased falls, further complicating the patient's health condition.

Therefore, it is crucial for caregivers and healthcare professionals working with dementia patients to be vigilant about signs of discomfort. Regularly assessing potential sources of pain - such as joint problems or dental issues - using validated tools designed specifically for people with cognitive impairments can help identify unreported pain.

Also important is creating an environment that minimizes potential causes of distress. This could involve ensuring a comfortable room temperature, providing soft clothing without hard fasteners or seams, and offering regular gentle exercise.

Recognizing and managing pain effectively should be an integral part of care strategies for people living with dementia. By doing so we can significantly improve their quality of life while potentially reducing some behavioral symptoms associated with this devastating disease.

Keep an eye out for non-verbal cues indicating discomfort such as grimacing or restlessness.

If you notice sudden changes in their behavior, it could be a sign of pain or discomfort due to an underlying medical issue. Always talk to healthcare professionals when you're unsure about something. There is undeniable value in exploring choice methods for pain management.

Non-pharmacological interventions can be effective in managing pain for dementia patients. This is especially important considering the fact that many traditional pain medications can have adverse side effects, particularly in older people. Incorporating such therapies into a comprehensive care plan could make all the difference when it comes to managing pain for someone with dementia. It's important not just to treat symptoms but also to enhance comfort and dignity during this challenging journey.

If you're caring for someone with dementia who is experiencing pain, consider exploring these choice therapies. They may not only provide relief from physical discomfort but also enhance emotional well-being and overall quality of life.

Finding the Right Medicine for Dementia

Walking down any pharmacy aisle or peering into the medicine section of a supermarket can be quite the sight—rows upon rows of various pills all promising relief from common health complaints. Just for stomach upsets alone, you'll see a bunch of options, not to mention several go-to choices for headaches, meds to slow down the runs, and others to help with the opposite problem. But when it comes to dementia, the shelf looks pretty bare. In reality, there are only four main medicines available, which are primarily used to manage Alzheimer's disease symptoms. The good news is that dementia is getting a lot of attention from governments and often hits the headlines, sparking hope that research into treatments will grow. Scientists and pharmaceutical companies are putting money into figuring out this complex condition, so fingers crossed for new breakthroughs in the future. Until then, we've got a simple rundown of what doctors have in their toolkit right now.

Keep in mind, these medicines aren't a cure for dementia, especially Alzheimer's disease, but they can help ease some symptoms. They focus on improving memory, thinking skills and also aim to help with emotional well-being and behavior. To make them as user-friendly as possible, they come in different forms like pills, skin patches, liquids, and dissolvable tabs.

Every drug has two names – a generic one, which is the standard name used by all manufacturers, and a brand name, which is unique to each drug company. Take ibuprofen for instance; that's the common name everyone can use, but when produced by Reckitt Benckiser, it's sold as Nurofen. The more makers out there, the more brand names you'll come across.

For those navigating the complexities of dementia medication, here's a list of the four drugs out there. We'll start with the generic names, followed by a few brand names you might recognize:

- Donepezil (brand names like Aricept)
- Rivastigmine (you might see it labeled Exelon, Kerstipon, or Nimvastid)
- Galantamine (goes by many names - Acumor, Elmino, Galantex, and others)
- Memantine (brand name Ebixa)

With this basic guide, we hope to offer not just information, but some comfort too. Remember, you're not alone on this path. There's a community and resources out there to provide support every step of the way. When someone has Alzheimer's disease, which is the most common type of dementia, their brain can't send messages as well as it should because they start to lose nerve cells. These nerve cells need a special chemical messenger called acetylcholine to talk to each other. Without enough of it, it's hard for a person to remember things or think straight, and they might feel and act differently than usual. Now, there are four medicines out there that help people with dementia, but they fit into two different groups based on how they help the brain.

Group One: Acetylcholinesterase Inhibitors

These drugs have long, fancy names like Donepezil, Rivastigmine, and Galantamine, but what they do is actually quite simple. They work against an enzyme—think of it as a little worker in your body—that breaks down acetylcholine. If this enzyme is blocked, you have more acetylcholine hanging around in the brain. This means nerve cells can chat better, and some symptoms of Alzheimer's can improve.

Group Two: Memantine

Memantine is all by itself in its group. It helps the brain in a different way. It deals with another brain chemical called glutamate, which is super important for learning and memory. This drug kind of acts like a guard, controlling how much calcium can enter the nerve cells. You see, when Alzheimer's disease is at work damaging brain cells, they go a bit overboard and release too much glutamate. This causes a flood of calcium into the cells which, unfortunately, can damage them even more. Memantine guards the cell to prevent too much calcium from getting in. This helps to protect the cells and slow down the progress of Alzheimer's.

Dealing with Alzheimer's is tough, but these medicines can offer a ray of hope. They work in their unique ways to help the brain do its job a little better and help those affected hold onto their memories and thinking abilities for longer. It's a complex battle, but understanding how these drugs work is one step towards supporting loved ones facing dementia.

Deciding When to Start Dementia Medication

Starting medication for dementia is a big decision that you'll make with your specialist's advice during your appointment. Your regular doctor (GP) may handle the actual prescription, but they will also keep an eye on how well the medication is working for you and look out for any side effects. You'll occasionally check back in with your specialist, too.

Before you begin any treatment, you need a formal diagnosis of dementia - your GP won't give you medication just to see if it might help without one. However, once you're diagnosed, and if the healthcare team feels it's the right choice for you, you'll likely start treatment immediately.

Here's what you need to know about the timing and choice of medication:

- **Acetylcholinesterase Inhibitors**: These are often the go-to drugs for mild to moderate Alzheimer's disease and can also be used for Lewy body disease or when someone has both Alzheimer's and vascular dementia. Your doctor will typically opt for the most cost-effective option first, making sure it's also safe and likely to work for you. Depending on how well the treatment works and if you're having any side effects, they can adjust your prescription as needed.
- **Memantine**: This medication isn't usually the first choice. It's often reserved for those who can't take acetylcholinesterase inhibitors due to adverse reactions or lack of response. It's approved for moderate to severe dementia and can be a next step if symptoms are serious. Plus, some studies show benefits when you combine it with your current medication.

Remember, every person's situation is unique, and your healthcare provider will guide you through the process to find the treatment that's best suited for you.

When it comes to dementia medication, there's quite a range to choose from. Usually, your doctor will start with a small dose and then, if necessary, gradually bump it up over time. We've put together a handy chart (you'll find it as Table 6) that lays out the different types of medication, how much to take, and how to take them for each of the four drugs commonly prescribed.

Table 7-1	Taking Dementia Medicines		
	Formats	Dose	Administration
Donepezil	Ordinary and melt-in-the-mouth tablets	5 mg initially; increased after 1 month to 10 mg	The same each day; ideally at bedtime
Rivastigmine	Tablets and patches	Tablets: 1.5 mg twice daily; can increase every 2 weeks in increments of 1.5 mg twice daily up to a maximum of 6 mg twice daily	Tablets: morning and evening
		Patches: start at 4.6 mg every 24 hours; can be increased after 4 weeks to a usual dose of 9.5 mg every 24 hours on a 14 day rotation	Patches: applied to non-hairy skin on the upper arms, chest or back; must be changed to a different position at the same time every 24 hours
Galantamine	Ordinary and the more commonly used modified tablets; liquid	Ordinary tablets and liquid: 4 mg once daily for at least 7 days; then 4 mg twice daily for at least 4 weeks, reaching maximum of 8 mg twice daily	Modified release tablets: morning
		Modified-release: start at 8 mg on alternate days for 7 days; then 8 mg once daily for 4 weeks, reaching maximum of 16 mg daily	Other preparations: same time each day; ideally morning and evening
Memantine	Tablets and liquid	Start on 5 mg once daily; can be increased weekly in 5-mg increments up to a maximum daily dose of 20 mg	Any time, but the same time each day

If you forget to take your medicine, don't worry – just skip the missed dose and continue as normal the next day, without taking extra. It's okay to keep using these medicines as long as they are helping you. According to the

Alzheimer's Society, many people – somewhere between 40 to 70 percent – see some improvement when they take these drugs. This improvement can last for about 6 to 12 months, and during this time, the progression of dementia might slow down a bit more than if they weren't taking any medication.

Considering Side Effects

It's true that no medication is perfect, and even the good ones might not be right for everybody. If you or a loved one are about to start on dementia meds, here are a few things to keep in mind.

Whenever you pick up a prescription, you'll find this paper inside that talks about side effects. These lists can be pretty long and scary, but don't worry too much just yet. Not everyone will get these side effects, and often the ones mentioned at the end of the list are pretty rare. Plus, starting off with a small dose can reduce your chances of experiencing any. You might feel some side effects when you first begin taking the medication, but usually, they chill out after a couple of days once your body gets the hang of it. If the side effects aren't too rough, hang in there for a bit and see if things get better.

Most folks on dementia drugs do just fine without much fuss. For example, side effects with memantine are not as common and tend to be more mild compared to those other ones called acetylcholinesterase inhibitors. But just so you're up to speed, here are some side effects that people might notice:

- **Acetylcholinesterase inhibitors:** You might not feel like eating, or you could feel sick, get an upset stomach, cramps, or diarrhea; sometimes people get headaches, feel dizzy or tired, or can't sleep; and watch out for skin reactions if you're using patches.
- **Memantine:** This one could also give you headaches, make you dizzy or tired; you might get constipated; sometimes it can make it tough to breathe, or affect your blood pressure.

And lastly, is there anyone who should steer clear of these drugs? Well:

- **Acetylcholinesterase inhibitors:** Almost everyone can take these, but if you're currently nursing a child (which is pretty rare if dementia's in the picture), then these may not be the best choice. Doctors tend to be cautious prescribing these if you've had issues with your heart, liver, lungs, kidneys, seizures, or if you're pregnant.
- **Memantine:** It's not the best fit if you're pregnant or if seizures are a thing for you. If you've got high blood pressure or problems with your heart, kidneys, or liver, or if you've had a recent heart attack, talk to your doc first.

Remember, medications are there to help, but they're one piece of the puzzle in managing dementia. It's all about finding what works best for you or your loved one, and that means being informed, staying alert to how you're feeling, and working closely with a healthcare provider who's got your back. Sometimes, doctors suggest medicine for other health problems to help people cope with dementia's tough symptoms. These meds are a mixed bag—some help, but they aren't for everyone or every type of dementia. Here's a quick lowdown on what's what.

Coping with Depression When You Have Dementia

It's pretty common for folks to feel depressed now and again, and it's no different for those living with dementia. Depression can look like being easily annoyed, not wanting to do fun stuff anymore, feeling down in the dumps, finding it hard to focus or remember, struggling to sleep or eat, crying easily, and sometimes thinking about death or worse.

When someone has dementia, adding depression to the mix is like a one-two punch that speeds up dementia problems. Treating depression can really turn things around and help people feel loads better.

How Antidepressants Help

These meds don't exactly put happy juice in your brain, but they pump up the good stuff—serotonin and noradrenaline—that seems to dip when you're feeling blue. It's more like they give your brain a leg up to get your own chemicals going stronger and make them work better. Usually, it takes a few weeks to start feeling better with antidepressants, and any pesky side effects typically come and go. If you've got to take them, it'll likely be for about four to six months. Don't sweat it; they're not the kind of meds that get you hooked.

When Do Doctors Recommend Antidepressants?

If your doctor thinks your case of the sads is more heavy-duty, they might bring up antidepressants. They don't just decide this out of the blue, and they won't reach for the script pad if you've just had a few bad days. Besides helping with the blues, these meds can also tone down worry and even perk you up a bit if life's been feeling blah.

Side Effects and Stuff to Watch For

Different meds come with different baggage. The most used ones for dementia are SSRIs and sometimes they can make you feel queasy, give you a stomachache, headache, make you tired, or mess with your appetite and love life. Your doctor will be extra careful if you have epilepsy, heart issues, diabetes, or a tendency to bleed in your gut. Also, they'll keep an eye out if you're taking strong pain meds like tramadol.

If you're caring for someone with dementia, you probably know how tough it can be for them to get a good night's sleep. It's tough on them and on caregivers too—there's the worry of them falling at night and the exhaustion everyone feels during the day. Some folks have trouble falling asleep, others wake up a lot during the night, and some deal with a mix of both.

Understanding Sleeping Pills

There are two main types of drugs doctors use to help with sleep, and they work a bit differently:

- **Benzodiazepines**
- **Z drugs** (they get this name because all their names start with "Z")

These drugs give a boost to a brain chemical called GABA (gamma-aminobutyric acid), which makes you feel sleepy and helps you nod off.

Sometimes, doctors might suggest other medications that aren't mainly for sleep but have drowsiness as a side effect. These could be certain antidepressants like trazodone, dosulepin, or amitriptyline, or even antihistamines like hydroxyzine.

For people over 55, there's also melatonin, a hormone our brains make to help control when we sleep and wake up. Taking a melatonin supplement can help kickstart sleep.

Knowing When Doctors Prescribe Sleeping Pills

Sleeping pills are not the first thing doctors turn to for treating sleep problems. They usually come into the picture only after other attempts haven't worked. This includes things like being more active during the day, cutting back on daytime naps, drinking less caffeine, and trying bright-light therapy (this uses special lights to help with the body's sleep-wake cycle).

Being Mindful of Side Effects and Risks

Sleeping pills can be habit-forming, so it's best not to use them for more than a couple of weeks. They're not a permanent fix. Plus, they can make you groggy, increase the chances of bathroom-related accidents, and cause unsteadiness that can lead to falls. They can also impact your breathing, which is why people with lung conditions or sleep apnoea need to steer clear of them.

Remember, dealing with sleep issues in dementia is tough, and it's important to find safe and practical ways to help everyone get the rest they need.

What Are Antipsychotic Medications?

Antipsychotic meds are a big help for those dealing with severe mental health troubles like schizophrenia. Back in the day, they changed the game by helping folks manage scary thoughts, paranoia, and hallucinations. Thanks to these meds, many can now live more everyday lives at home, rather than being stuck in asylums. Some antipsychotics can also calm hallucinations and confusion in people with dementia. They can even ease feelings of aggression and help people feel less upset.

How Do Antipsychotic Drugs Work?

Antipsychotics come in two main kinds – old-school ones like chlorpromazine and newer options like risperidone. Newer ones have been around since the 1970s and tend to be easier on your system. These drugs tackle neurotransmitters in our brains. Serotonin, noradrenaline, and acetylcholine are all part of the mix, but dopamine is the big one they go after.

When Do Doctors Prescribe Antipsychotics?

Docs don't just hand out these drugs like candy. They reserve them for when someone's behavior or psychological symptoms get really tough to manage. Even though they work for about half the people who take them, docs won't prescribe them for long—just about 12 weeks—and they keep a close eye on their patients for any harsh side effects.

What About Side Effects?

Like all drugs, antipsychotics can cause side effects. Since they play around with lots of neurotransmitters, the effects can vary. For example, dopamine is linked to movement, so some people might feel shakier or have trouble staying steady, which can increase the chance of falling. Other issues could be headaches, feeling wiped out, or stomach problems.

People with heart issues need to be careful with these meds, and they're a no-go for folks with Lewy body disease. That's because half the people with this condition react badly to antipsychotics—it can make things worse and, in some cases, can be really dangerous.

Why Do Drugs Have Side Effects Anyway?

When we pop a pill, we're basically introducing something our bodies aren't used to, and sometimes it can cause trouble. Thankfully, severe reactions are rare considering how often prescriptions are written. But even the small side effects can be annoying. People can experience side effects for different reasons. It might be an allergy, which can get serious, or intolerance, which usually affects the stomach or head. Some folks might break down drugs slower, others might have health conditions that affect how drugs work in their system. Also, as we age, our bodies don't get rid of drugs as efficiently. Sometimes the drug itself is the issue because, while they're meant to target specific cells, they can end up affecting other parts of the body too, leading to side effects we don't want. Drugs also don't always play nice with each other, meaning if you're taking more than one, they could interact and cause side effects.

Understanding these medications and their side effects can help us make better choices and have more empathy for those who rely on them. Remember, it's about finding balance – managing symptoms while keeping an eye on how the treatment is affecting overall health. It's a delicate dance that requires compassion and knowledge.

Chapter 13

Considering Natural Treatments

In This Section:

- Discovering the benefits of herbs and vitamins
- Enhancing well-being through aromatherapy
- Exploring treatments that make life feel more real

There's a whole bunch of treatments for dementia that your doctor won't scribble on a prescription pad. Some folks call them complementary or alternative therapies, and there's a mixed bag—it's not all created equal! Sadly, there's also a fair share of hogwash floating around. Pop "alternative medicine + dementia" into Google, and you'll find all sorts of wild recipes that sound like they're straight out of a fantasy novel.

Despite that, I've talked to many folks who tell me they've seen the real deal—a friend or family member getting better at remembering stuff after taking some plant extract or vitamin pill. And as an open-minded person, I'm not about to put my foot down on something that just might help, even if it hasn't got the science to back it up fully (as long as we know it's not harmful).

In this section, I'm laying out a straight-up rundown on some popular natural treatments for dementia symptoms. We're talking about remedies that use plants, vitamins, or a mix of both, as well as hands-on, practical therapy types. Now, when it comes to the hard evidence that these alternative options actually work—well, sometimes it's pretty thin on the ground, not as solid as with the stuff you get from the pharmacy. Still, I'm not here to discourage anyone from giving them a go if they're safe. That said, I'm a firm believer in not skipping out on doctor-recommended treatments. Those are tried and true pathways that have been shown to truly make a difference.

For thousands of years, people have turned to plants and herbs for healing. They're still pretty popular today, where there's a big trend to go natural for health fixes. Even for conditions like dementia, some herbs get a lot of buzz for their potential soothing powers. Here's the lowdown on these natural remedies, where they come from, what they're believed to do, and a reality check on whether they actually work. Remember, just because something is labeled 'natural,' it doesn't mean it's totally safe or won't mix badly with other meds you might be taking.

Gingko Biloba: The All-Star of Herbal Remedies

When we're talking about herbs for dementia, gingko biloba often steals the show. A lot of people swear by it, and if you poke around online, you'll notice it's almost mainstream.

This special plant comes from the gingko tree, also known as the maidenhair tree, which has been around since the dinosaurs roamed the earth! You can find these trees all over, but they're especially common in China and Japan. Fun fact: The oldest of these trees lived for 3,500 years.

What's the Secret Inside Gingko Leaves?

Turns out, gingko leaves are packed with compounds called flavonoids and terpenoids. Flavonoids are like nature's rust protectors for your body, mainly helping your nervous system, while terpenoids are great for blood flow—they widen blood vessels and stop blood cells from clumping up into clots.

People think gingko biloba is a hit because it keeps brain cells safe and the blood pumping. That's why some suggest it could be a buddy for folks with Alzheimer's or vascular dementia by:

- Making memory better
- Lifting one's spirits and keeping the blues at bay
- Helping with everyday stuff like socializing and grabbing groceries

Free Radicals: Not as Fun as They Sound

Despite the cool name, free radicals aren't rebel atoms fighting a war. Instead, they're atoms that are missing a buddy electron. This makes them super desperate and they end up stealing electrons from other molecules, turning them into free radicals too. Like dominos, this can lead to a big mess.

Inside us, these wild free radicals can wreck cells, and even tamper with our DNA, which might cause diseases. In dementia, when brain cells get messed up, that's the main issue.

Free radicals happen naturally in our bodies, but stuff like pollution and smoking can make more of them too. The good thing is our bodies have their own superheroes called antioxidants that neutralize free radicals.

To boost your antioxidant power, munch on these good-for-you foods:

- Berries like strawberries, blackberries, blueberries, and raspberries
- Fruits such as grapes, cherries, plums, bananas, kiwi, and pineapple
- Veggies including kale, red cabbage, broccoli, asparagus, potatoes, and tomatoes
- Nuts like pistachios, walnuts, pecans, and hazelnuts

Eating your fruits and veggies isn't just tasty—it's your body's natural armor against those pesky free radicals. And that's why folks are into the idea of getting an extra health kick from herbal and vitamin therapies.

Side Effects of Gingko

Gingko is usually pretty safe to take, but like anything else you might try for your health, it can cause a few side effects. Sometimes you might get an upset stomach, a skin rash, feel dizzy, or get a headache.

There's something important you should know about gingko, though. It affects how your blood clots by making platelets less sticky. This means if you're going to have surgery, you should stop taking gingko a couple of days before so you don't bleed too much.

Gingko can also mess with some other medicines you might be taking:

- **For seizures:** If you're on medicine for epilepsy, like carbamazepine or sodium valproate, gingko could make them work less well, which means you could have more seizures.
- **For depression:** If you're taking SSRIs (things like citalopram, sertraline, fluoxetine, or paroxetine), then mixing them with gingko could cause

serotonin syndrome. This is serious and can give you symptoms like high blood pressure, a heartbeat that's way too fast, sweating a lot, shaking, stiff muscles, overactive reflexes, feeling anxious or worked up, and in really bad cases, a coma. You really want to avoid this one.

- **For high blood pressure:** Since gingko makes your blood vessels expand, it can lower your blood pressure. This could be dangerous if you're already taking medicine for high blood pressure because it might lower it too much.
- **For blood clotting:** Blood thinners like warfarin, aspirin or clopidogrel can get more powerful with gingko, and that could be risky.

Does Gingko Actually Work?

Well, it looks promising! A big study in Germany with more than 2,000 people showed that gingko extract did help with dementia symptoms compared to a placebo. But when they looked at gingko versus other dementia meds, the other drugs worked better.

A 20-year study from Bordeaux saw a bit of hope - gingko seemed to slow down the brain's aging process in healthy older adults. Yet, other scientists say that gingko doesn't really stop dementia from happening.

Gingko isn't a miracle cure for dementia, and it's not going to replace medicines that doctors prescribe for it. But for people who don't have issues with the other meds we talked about, trying gingko might be something to consider.

Vitamin E - A Natural Boost or Not?

Lots of folks these days are turning to nature, hoping to find healthier ways to fight illness. This has made vitamins really popular, and they are often sold with big promises to cure a bunch of different health issues. For brain health problems like dementia, people say vitamin E is pretty amazing.

Vitamin E is a good guy found in things that grow – like fruits, veggies, and certain oils. It's better to get this vitamin from the food you eat rather than swallowing it in pill form. You can find vitamin E in:

- Sunflower and olive oils
- Nuts like almonds and hazelnuts
- Fruits such as kiwi and mangoes, and veggies like tomatoes
- More veggies like pumpkin, turnip, and sweet potatoes, along with avocados and asparagus
- Fish and shellfish

With such a fantastic lineup of foods, it's easy to see why people think vitamin E is beneficial.

This vitamin is also like a bodyguard for the skin of our cells, keeping them healthy and working right.

What Makes Vitamin E Special?

Just like with the herb gingko, experts think the real star in vitamin E is something called antioxidants.

Potential Downsides

But, hear this, just because it's all-natural and in yummy stuff like kiwi, doesn't mean vitamin E can't have a downside when you take too much of it concentrated in a pill. Some problems you might run into are feeling sick, getting diarrhea, or feeling weak in the muscles.

And if you're taking medicine to keep your blood thin, like warfarin, adding lots of vitamin E could make you bleed or bruise more easily. What's scarier is that some studies say if you take too much vitamin E for a long time, it could actually up your chances of dying from something.

What Does the Research Say?

A lot of studies on vitamin E were done on animals, but a big research study in 2014 had people take either vitamin E, a dementia drug called memantine, both of them together, or just a dummy pill. They found that vitamin E did help people keep doing their everyday things a bit longer compared to those who took the dummy pill. But taking both vitamin E and the dementia drug didn't work better than just vitamin E alone. However, there's still worry about whether it's safe to take the high amounts of vitamin E they used in the study for a long time.

For Now, What Should You Do?

While it's tempting to try vitamin E, because we don't know all the risks, it's probably safer to stick with other treatments that doctors know more about at the moment.

For centuries, Huperzine A has been a key part of traditional Chinese medicine, known for its ability to improve memory and reduce inflammation. This natural extract comes from a plant called fir clubmoss, which grows in India and Southeast Asia.

What Exactly is Huperzine A?

Huperzine A works somewhat like over-the-counter drugs that help with memory problems because it has certain chemical properties. Essentially, it latches onto an enzyme that usually breaks down a substance in our brain that's necessary for memory. When Huperzine A gets in the way, this substance sticks around longer and may aid in better brain function.

A Heads-Up on Side Effects

Although Huperzine A can be helpful, it's not all smooth sailing. Some folks may experience:

- Tightness in the chest or throat
- A slower pulse
- Stomach issues like pain, diarrhea, or feeling queasy
- Trouble sleeping

And it's wise to steer clear of Huperzine A if you're pregnant, breastfeeding, or a child. If you're already taking meds for memory issues or dementia, adding Huperzine A to the mix might not be a good idea. It's also worth noting that for those with glaucoma, Huperzine A could worsen things by reducing the effectiveness of their existing treatments.

The Research Says...

There's some preliminary research that shows potential with Huperzine A improving memory and lessening the negative impacts of dementia. Yet, we don't have enough solid proof to recommend it as a go-to treatment. That's mostly because there are already tried-and-tested drugs available that not only work in similar ways but are also verified to be safe.

Beyond Conventional Medicine

When we talk about non medical treatments, we often hear terms like "alternative" or "complementary" therapies. There's a whole bunch of practitioners in this space—like osteopaths, homeopaths, and herbalists—with various levels of regulation. If you're thinking about going down this route, you'll want to ensure whoever you see is legit.

A good place to start is the Complementary and Natural Healthcare Council's registry. They only list professionals who meet strict standards of practice and ethics.

But remember, the term "complementary" is intentional. While these therapies can work alongside traditional medicine, they're not replacements. Doctors and healthcare teams rely on treatments that have been rigorously tested to be both safe and effective. Sure, they might come with side effects, but they're proven to be safe when used properly.

VITACOG

VITACOG is the catchy name for a special mix of B vitamins – that's B6, B12, and folic acid – whipped up by smart folks at Oxford University. They wanted to see if this combo might slow down how quickly people with dementia lose their thinking skills. It's been in the news a lot, and lots of people are talking about it. Now, the scientists mixed up their own special batch for the study, but you can actually find these super-important B vitamins in ordinary foods like:

- **B6**: This one's in chicken, pork, fish, cereal, rice, eggs, milk, potatoes, soybeans, and loads of veggies.
- **B12**: Look for it in beef, fish, dairy stuff (like milk, eggs, and cheese), and cereals that say they've got extra vitamins.
- **Folic Acid**: Green machine! It's in broccoli, Brussels sprouts, spinach, peas, chickpeas, those same fortifed cereals, and liver.

These vitamins are the heroes in VITACOG – they get down to business by taking down something called homocysteine. Your body gets more of this amino acid as you get older, and too much of it can harm your brain cells. This damage can actually make your brain smaller and mess with your memory and how well you can think.

Good news – the B vitamins in VITACOG are three little warriors fighting to lower the homocysteine in your body to keep your brain safe from harm. While VITACOG doesn't really have bad side effects, it might not play nice with iron pills or blood thinning meds, so keep that in mind. When it comes to proof, things are looking up. Those taking part in the Oxford study had less brain shrinkage when they lowered their homocysteine. But the jury's still out on whether this can actually ease dementia symptoms or keep dementia from getting worse. The smart folks in lab coats have more work to do.

Medical Foods for Dementia

There's quite a buzz around special foods designed to combat dementia, especially Alzheimer's disease, and they've been getting lots of attention in the news. Think of them like special milkshakes with a mission. Souvenaid and Axona are two products leading the way. These drinks aren't your typical smoothies—they're packed with a mix of nutrients intended to protect brain cells and help sharpen your memory and thinking skills.

Nutricia's Souvenaid boasts a cocktail of ingredients aimed at supporting nerve cells in the brain. Here's what's in it:

- Omega 3 fish oils that our brains just love
- Phospholipids, key building blocks for our brain cells
- Choline, important for brain health
- A bundle of B vitamins (folic acid, B6, B12), along with vitamins C and E
- Selenium, a mineral with antioxidant powers

All these ingredients work together to help people with Alzheimer's rebuild connections between their brain cells, fight off the damage caused by the illness, and cut down on troubling symptoms. Now, Axona takes a different approach. It's almost like a one-man band with its main ingredient—caprylic triglyceride from coconut oil. The idea is to give the brain an alternative energy source when it can't use its usual favorite, glucose.

Both these milkshakes are pretty gentle on the body, but they can sometimes cause minor discomfort like tummy troubles, a feeling of nausea, and a touch of gas. Axona, in particular, should be taken carefully by those managing diabetes. Scientifically speaking, some small studies have noticed improvements in memory and thinking for folks with mild dementia who tried Souvenaid and Axona. However, they do come with a hefty price tag, and you can't get them on prescription, so it's worth weighing up whether the benefits are worth the cost.

Aromatherapy

Aromatherapy isn't a new fad—it's been around for ages. People have enjoyed the benefits of scented oils since at least 3000 BC, long before they even started writing about it. These oils weren't just sniffed for pleasure; ancient Egyptians, Greeks, and Romans used them to treat all sorts of ailments. Fast-forward to today, and there's a whole world of over 400 essential oils people use regularly. Each oil is special, with its own way of helping our minds and bodies feel better.

For those dealing with dementia, certain oils might offer a bit of comfort:

- Basil
- Chamomile
- Coriander
- Lavender
- Lemon and lemon balm
- Neroli

These scents have been singled out because they're believed to soothe and provide some relief. Whether you're caring for someone with dementia or simply curious about the healing power of scents, it's good to know that these fragrant drops can make a difference.

Aromatherapists really look at the big picture when they work with someone. First off, they get to know their clients really well, asking about their health history and what's been bothering them. Then they come up with a game plan, picking out just the right essential oils to help.

The way these oils get to do their magic can happen in quite a few ways:

- **Massage:** They might rub the oils right into your skin.
- **Baths:** Sometimes, adding a couple of drops to bathwater does the trick so it touches your skin and you breathe in all the goodness too.
- **Inhalations and vaporizers:** Think of it like a gentle, scented smoke that you breathe in, often with candles around.
- **Compresses:** This is all about putting the oils exactly where you've got pain or an injury.

Now, as for how it all works, aromatherapists have this idea that the tiny oil particles sneak into your body through your skin or when you breathe them in, zip through your bloodstream, and get busy healing by messing with hormones and stuff. Scientists are on the fence, though. The top guess is that your sense of smell plays a huge role. The scents tickle receptors in your nose, which sends signals all the way to your brain's emotion and memory center. Then your brain lights up and releases its own feel-good chemicals that help you chill out. It sounds about right, doesn't it? Sure, the proof isn't rock solid yet. But some brainy folks have noticed that smells can ease restlessness and make people less upset – and that's a big deal for those dealing with dementia. That's why even though we don't have all the answers, giving aromatherapy a chance isn't such a bad idea. Keep in mind that some people have had serious reactions on their skin when using oils.

Reminiscing for Wellness

There's something special about sharing good memories with friends and family. For me, it's all about the '80s. A quick glance at TV clips or listening to a classic tune from that time, and I'm all smiles. I love remembering– Members Only jackets, slim ties, straight-legged trousers, high hair, and poofy sleeves. And if a song by Journey or Depeche Mode comes on the radio, I'm right back in those happy days. Reminiscence therapy is all about accessing these treasured memories. Bringing back the sights, sounds, tastes, and even smells from the good old days can make life brighter for someone who's struggling with the present. This approach isn't just nostalgic; it can genuinely lift the spirits of someone with dementia, and improve their overall wellbeing, helping them stay connected with caregivers, friends, and family. Plus, it can even give a little boost to their brain function.

But it's not just about the good times, either. Sometimes, a walk down memory lane might bring up painful memories or remind someone of a loss they're still grieving. It's important to handle these memories with care and support the person as they express their feelings – even if that means having a heartfelt cry. It's worth noting that reminiscence therapy isn't for everyone. People should always have a choice in participating, as it's only helpful when it's welcomed.

The beauty of reminiscence therapy lies in its endless possibilities—you can tailor it to individuals or groups and adapt it to various environments like homes, day centers, care facilities, and hospitals. For a trip down memory lane, you can use anything from photographs and home movies to favourite snacks and music. Creating a scrapbook is a fun way to keep the stories alive and to revisit those memorable moments over and over again.

Here are some ideas to stimulate the senses:

Sound: Music is the gateway to our past. Whether it's a song from a first date, a wedding dance, or just a theme from a much-loved film, revisiting this music can spark lively discussions about the special people and events associated with those tunes.

Touch: Sometimes just holding something precious, like a piece of jewelry or a well-loved ornament, opens up a world of stories – say, where it came from or who gave it to them. Even old clothes, medals, or trophies can summon up a mix of emotions and memories.

Sight: Flipping through old photo albums or watching vintage films can prompt remembrance too. Books filled with pictures from someone's hometown or watching newsreels from big events in history might also stir up fond memories.

Taste and Smell: Sharing a nostalgic meal or aroma can evoke thoughts of past experiences or loved ones. Involve them in preparing a favorite dish or recreate a dining out scene, and you can encourage conversations about happy moments spent with others. Contrary to how this may sound, this isn't about escaping reality, but enriching the present with the warmth of the past. When done with sensitivity, reminiscence therapy blends cherished yesterdays into brighter todays for those who need it most.

Music Therapy

Sometimes a song just hits you right in the feels, doesn't it? Whether it's the tune, the lyrics, or a memory tied to it, music has this amazing ability to make us feel all sorts of emotions, from deep sadness to uncontrolled happiness. Ever found yourself spontaneously crying to a ballad or dancing around your room like nobody's watching, singing into your hairbrush? Well, you're not alone! Just like individual experiences with music can make us sentimental or hyped up, it's incredible how music can connect groups of people too. Ever felt that special bond singing hymns in a church or belting out the lyrics with your favorite band under the open sky at a music festival? Yeah, that's the magic of music.

With music therapy, this emotional magic is put to work to help improve people's wellbeing. It's not just about listening to music – joining in and making music with instruments or voices can be just as powerful.

Music and the Brain

Ever wonder how far back in time music goes? Well, music is literally as old as humanity and is found in every culture on the planet. Our ancestors probably sang tunes and played instruments by the fire in the African Rift Valley ages ago! Archaeologists even dug up old flutes made from bones in Germany that are over 35,000 years old. These ancient instruments tell us that music has always been part of who we are. But why do we love music so much, especially when it doesn't really help us survive like food or shelter? Enter Robert Zatorre, a cool neuroscientist at McGill University in Canada, who's been trying to figure this out. His team uses fancy brain scans and found that when we get goosebumps from our favorite songs, our brains release dopamine – the same chemical that makes us feel good when we eat our favorite food or fall in love. It's what makes music so rewarding.

We're just beginning to scratch the surface in understanding how music affects our brains. But, for someone with dementia, music can unlock memories that they can't access any other way. Knowing this, it seems less surprising how music and singing can be such a healing experience for many.

Music for Dementia

Music truly has a magical touch, a medical conference in 2013 was a topic about how the human voice can heal, and we were shown this heart-touching video of an elderly lady with Alzheimer's, who I'll call Marjorie. Marjorie, 80 years old, was deep into Alzheimer's clutches. She needed people for everything and had stopped mingling or even talking to anyone at the care home. It had been weeks since she uttered a single word. Yet, she welcomed a music therapist who visited her.

The video started with the therapist in her room, gently playing his guitar. He played old tunes that Marjorie probably heard in her youth. Before long, something amazing happened. Marjorie, who hadn't spoken in forever, started to make noises. It was not precisely singing, and the tune was off, but it was rhythmic, in line with the music. For the first time in forever, she was reaching out and connecting through music. We were glued to the screen, witnessing this miracle, and I guess there wasn't one person without tears in that room. Music reached a part of Marjorie that Alzheimer's couldn't touch. It gave her a voice and, for those brief moments, she was vibrant and alive again.

The video ended with Marjorie falling silent again, and she sadly passed away shortly after that. It was the last time anyone heard her voice. This showed us the two ways music therapy can work:

- **Receptive therapy:** where people listen to the therapist play and sing.
- **Active therapy:** which encourages people to sing along and play simple instruments.

Music isn't just sound; it's a bridge to forgotten lands, especially for people like Marjorie. It reaffirms the power of music in healing and connecting us in the most unexpected ways.

Understanding Reality Orientation for Dementia

Imagine you wake up one morning in a place that's not your bedroom. The walls are painted in unfamiliar colors, there's artwork you've never seen before, and even the clock isn't where it's supposed to be. It's disorienting to wake up somewhere new, but usually, within a few moments, you remember you're at a hotel or a friend's house, and the feeling fades.

Now, think about how this sensation would feel if it didn't go away – if every morning, you struggled to remember where you are or even what day it is. This is the daily reality for someone living with dementia. Constantly feeling lost is understandably upsetting and can cause a great deal of stress.

This is where the concept of reality orientation comes in. It's a gentle yet powerful way to help someone with dementia ground themselves in the here and now. By anchoring them to who they are, who's around them, where they are, and the time, it can greatly reduce their confusion.

Here are some ways to help someone with dementia feel more oriented:

- Place a board in a common area with the day, date, time, and weather – don't forget to update it daily.

- Install large clocks in each room for an easy time reference.
- Buy a newspaper every day to keep up with current events – and recycle the old ones promptly.
- Label each door with its room purpose to prevent mix-ups.
- In care settings, ensure everyone wears a nametag to avoid identity confusion.
- Talk about recent news stories, use the individual's name often in conversation, and refer regularly to the current day of the week.

By incorporating these changes, you can create a supportive environment that lends a sense of normalcy and reduces agitation for people with dementia. Understanding and patience go a long way, and simple efforts can make a world of difference.

The Upsides

Studies have shown that reality orientation, when it goes hand in hand with dementia medication, can actually do a lot of good. Take this 2005 study from the British Journal of Psychiatry. It found that people who tried reality orientation therapy for 25 weeks did better on memory and other brain tests compared to those who just took medication. Plus, it seems like reality orientation helps folks interact better socially.

But, we've got to take these findings with a grain of salt. The studies were pretty small, so we can't say for sure these results would happen for everyone. Yet, the Cochrane Library tossed in their two cents in 2003, saying there's enough good vibes coming from reality orientation therapy that it's worth giving it a shot.

The Downsides

Not everyone's sold on reality orientation though. Some worry that constantly correcting someone with dementia—reminding them where they are or what the date is—could actually stress them out more. Imagine how tough it would be to be told over and over that your spouse passed away, especially if you keep forgetting that heartbreak. Or, think about how annoying it would be if someone was always on your case about minor slip-ups.

Looking at Alternatives

Because some folks questioned reality orientation, other approaches have popped up:

- **Validation therapy**: This one's all about the emotional side, not just the facts. If someone with dementia is upset waiting for a parent who's no longer here, instead of saying "They passed away," a caregiver might say "They're running late" and find a way to distract or comfort them. It has its perks, but the jury's still out on whether it's the go-to solution for everyone.

- **Specialised Early Care for Alzheimer's (SPECAL)**: Penny Garner whipped this up while caring for her mom with dementia. The aim here is to keep things chill so that no one gets upset trying to remember things that their mind won't help them with. Basically, the approach follows three rules:
  - No tricky questions.
  - Listen to what people with dementia have to say—they know best.

o   Don't correct them.

It can really help cut down on the stress for those living with dementia and their caregivers. But, some critics think it's not great for people in the early stages because it doesn't include them in decisions—something organizations like the Alzheimer's Society consider mega important.

The Takeaway

Every therapy has its pros and cons. They can definitely help a bunch of people and their caregivers. Since everyone's different, sickness or not, it makes sense to test out these methods. See what works for the person you're caring for. Tailored care is usually the most successful. It's like clothes—custom-fit usually beats ready-made.

Chapter 14:

The Unsung Heroes

Welcome aboard my fellow unsung heroes! Let's unveil the curtain on taking care of ourselves while caring for our loved ones with dementia. After all, every caregiver deserves their own share of care too.

This journey will not be easy; there will be days filled with exhaustion and frustration, moments when you feel helpless or isolated. But let me tell you something: taking care of yourself isn't selfish—it's essential! You cannot pour from an empty cup. It's okay to prioritize your well-being, it's okay to take a break, and most importantly, it's okay to ask for help.

My hope is that you will find solace in knowing you are not alone. And maybe, just maybe, you'll feel a little less overwhelmed and a bit more equipped to handle this challenging role.

So, here are 5 strategies for maintaining health as a dementia caregiver I have learned while taking care of a loved one with dementia.

1) Regular Exercise:

Regular exercise is not only useful for the physical health of caregivers, but also for their mental well-being. In particular, those caring for individuals with dementia can experience high levels of stress and burnout.

According to a study published in the Journal of Alzheimer's Disease, caregivers who engaged in regular physical activity reported lower levels of stress and depressive symptoms compared to those who did not exercise regularly. This suggests that maintaining an active lifestyle can help mitigate some of the emotional strain associated with caregiving.

Research from the University of Pittsburgh found that moderate-intensity exercise can lead to improved sleep quality among dementia caregivers. Given that poor sleep is a common issue among this group due to nighttime disruptions caused by patients' behavioral issues, incorporating regular exercise into their routine could be a practical strategy for improving sleep patterns.

It's crucial as a caregiver to make time for regular physical activity - whether it's going for a brisk walk around the block or engaging in a yoga session at home. Not only will this help keep you physically fit and better equipped to handle your caregiving duties, but it will also provide much-needed respite from the emotional challenges you face daily.

2) Balanced Diet: Proper nutrition fuels our bodies' functions including our mental capacity.

Maintaining a balanced diet is not only crucial for physical health, but also for mental well-being. This advice is particularly pertinent to caregivers who are looking after patients with dementia.

According to a study published in the American Journal of Clinical Nutrition, a diet rich in fruits, vegetables, lean proteins and whole grains can significantly reduce the risk of cognitive decline and improve overall brain function.

The antioxidants found in these foods protect brain cells from damage and support the growth of new ones.

For caregivers, this means that maintaining a balanced diet could potentially enhance their ability to care for their loved ones suffering from dementia. Not only does it keep them physically healthy and energetic, but it also helps them stay mentally sharp and focused on their caregiving tasks.

Studies have shown that caregivers often experience high levels of stress which can lead to poor dietary choices. By prioritizing their own nutritional needs alongside those of the person they're caring for, caregivers can better manage this stress and maintain optimal health.

Prioritize a balanced diet filled with nutrient-rich foods to confirm you're at your best both physically and mentally while providing care.

3) Adequate Rest: Chronic sleep deprivation can lead to serious health problems including depression and a weakened immune system.

Caregivers for dementia patients, who are often under immense stress and strain, can significantly benefit from proper rest and sleep.

A study conducted by the University of California found that caregivers who had poor sleep quality showed higher levels of depression and caregiver burden. In contrast, those who managed to maintain a healthy sleep schedule experienced lower stress levels and better overall health.

A lack of adequate rest can lead to impaired cognitive function, which could potentially affect the quality of care provided to the dementia patient. Sleep deprivation has been linked with decreased attention span, slower reaction times, and increased risk of errors - all factors that can negatively impact caregiving tasks.

While caring for a loved one with dementia is indeed challenging, it's important not to neglect your own needs. Try setting a regular sleep schedule or engaging in relaxing activities before bedtime such as reading or taking a warm bath. If you're finding it difficult to manage your responsibilities and get enough rest, don't hesitate to seek help from support groups or professional services.

Aim for 7-9 hours of sleep per night. If finding a continuous block of time is challenging because of caregiving duties, try incorporating short naps into your routine.

4) Social Connections: Maintaining relationships outside your caregiving role is crucial for emotional wellbeing.

According to a study published in the Journal of Gerontology, caregivers who have strong social networks report less stress and better overall mental health than those who are socially isolated. The study found that these caregivers were not only able to manage their caregiving duties more effectively but also experienced fewer symptoms of depression.

Caring for someone with dementia can be an emotionally taxing experience. It's easy to become overwhelmed by the demands of caregiving and neglect your own needs, including the need for social interaction. However, it's important to remember that you don't have to go through this journey alone.

The benefits of having a robust social network are manifold: from emotional support and advice from others who may be going through similar experiences, to practical help such as sharing care responsibilities or providing respite care.

Another study in Aging & Mental Health suggests that engaging in regular social activities can even slow cognitive decline among caregivers themselves. This means staying socially active could not only improve your mental health but also keep your mind sharp.

Regular interactions with friends or family members provide opportunities to share experiences, gain perspective, and simply enjoy life beyond caregiving.

So, whether it's joining a local support group, catching up with friends over coffee or even just chatting on the phone with family members - make sure you're taking time out of your busy schedule to connect with others.

5) Professional Help: Don't hesitate to seek professional help if feelings of stress or anxiety become overwhelming.

Scientific studies suggest that seeking professional help when caring for a loved one with dementia can have significant benefits, not only for the patient but also for the caregiver.

According to a study published in the Journal of Geriatric Psychiatry and Neurology, caregivers who received professional support experienced lower levels of stress and depression. The study further revealed that these caregivers were able to provide better care which resulted in improved quality of life for the dementia patients.

Caring for someone with dementia is challenging and can be overwhelming. It involves managing symptoms such as memory loss, confusion, difficulty communicating, mood changes, and problems with day-to-day tasks. This responsibility often leads to caregiver burnout characterized by physical, emotional, and mental exhaustion.

However, professionals trained in dementia care are equipped with skills to manage these challenges effectively. They understand the disease progression and can provide interventions tailored to each stage. They also offer respite to family caregivers allowing them time to rest and recharge.

Research conducted by Alzheimer's Association shows that early diagnosis through professional help allows more time for critical care planning which significantly improves patient outcomes.

When you engage professionals in your caregiving journey, you're not just ensuring better care for your loved one but also preserving your own health and well-being. Remember it's not about replacing your role as a caregiver but enhancing it so you can continue providing love and support while maintaining balance in your life.

Taking care of yourself is a must to maintain the quality of care for your loved one. Don't be afraid to take care of the things you need for yourself.

Chapter 15:

Hospice, Respite, and Full-care facilities

Taking care of an elderly or disabled family member is never easy, you may need a break from your day-to-day responsibilities as a caregiver. Respite care may be an option for you.

Respite care is an opportunity for a caregiver to receive assistance from a temporary care facility for an elderly, ill, or handicapped individual or family member. Whether it is for a few hours a week or for an entire year, respite care can help you keep your life in balance while caring for your family member.

Respite care can be provided at home, or in a care setting, such as a residential facility or adult day care. Services provided at home offer a range of options including:

- Personal care to provide help with bathing, dressing, and exercising.

- Supervision of activities and outings

- Medication management

- Assistance with laundry, shopping, and preparing meals.

Adult day care centers are places where your family member can go to be looked after while you run errands. Adult day care provides a safe and social environment for an elderly or disabled family member to visit for a few hours or a full day. Residential facilities may provide an opportunity for an overnight stay if you are on vacation or need an extended break.

Respite care not only provides an opportunity for you to recharge your batteries, but it will give you peace of mind knowing your loved one is being cared for in your absence.

Respite care can provide opportunities for social interaction and engagement in a safe environment. A study from Aging & Mental Health showed that dementia patients participating in day-care programs exhibited improved cognitive function and mood.

Therefore, it's important to consider incorporating respite care into your caregiving plan if you're looking after someone with dementia. It's not just about taking a break - it's about ensuring optimal health for both yourself as a caregiver and the person you're caring for.

Keep in mind, Medicare may only pay for respite care if the person you are caring for has a life-threatening illness and qualifies for hospice benefits. Be sure to discuss respite care with your family member's insurance carrier.

Hospice care

Hospice care is end-of-life care. It is provided by a team of health care professionals and volunteers. They give medical, psychological, and spiritual support. Hospice care can significantly improve the quality of life for dementia patients, especially in their final stages.

Usually, a hospice patient is expected to live 6 months or less. Hospice care can take place:

- At home

- At a hospice center

- In a hospital

- In a skilled nursing facility

According to a study published in the Journal of American Geriatrics Society, dementia patients receiving hospice care were less likely to be hospitalized or die in a hospital, and more likely to receive adequate pain management compared to those not receiving hospice care.

Hospice care focuses on comfort rather than cure, which aligns with the needs of advanced dementia patients who often suffer from distressing symptoms such as agitation, difficulty swallowing and pain. Controlling pain and other symptoms can help a person remain alert and as comfortable as possible. This approach is useful as it reduces unnecessary hospitalizations and interventions that may not improve or could even worsen their quality of life. Hospice care helps people who are dying have peace, comfort, and dignity.

Moreover, hospice teams are skilled at providing emotional support to both the patient and their family members. They help families understand what's happening medically with their loved one and guide them through difficult decisions about treatment options.

Full-time care facilities

According to a study published in the Journal of American Geriatrics Society, patients with dementia who are placed in full-time care facilities often experience better health outcomes than those who remain at home. This is largely due to the round-the-clock medical attention and professional care they receive, which is difficult to replicate in a home setting.

The same study also highlighted that caregivers of dementia patients often suffer from high levels of stress and burnout. Moving your loved one into a full care facility not only confirms they get the best possible care but also gives you as a caregiver some much-needed respite.

However, it's important to note that this transition can be stressful for both you and your loved one. Therefore, experts recommend taking time to prepare for this change. Visit various facilities before making your choice, ask plenty of questions about the level of care provided, and involve your loved one in the decision-making process as much as possible.

Also remember that feelings of guilt or sadness are normal during this period. It might help to join support groups or seek counseling services where you can share experiences with others going through similar situations.

While moving a loved one with dementia into full-time care may be challenging emotionally, science shows us that it could lead to better health outcomes for them and less stress for you. It's all about finding balance between ensuring their safety and maintaining their dignity throughout this process.

Scientific research has shown that specialized care facilities for dementia patients can provide numerous benefits over hospice care at home. This is not to say that hospice care isn't useful, but rather, it's about understanding the unique needs of a person with dementia and how these needs can be best met.

A study published in the Journal of American Geriatrics Society found that dementia patients in full-care facilities had better health outcomes compared to those receiving hospice care at home. These facilities are equipped with staff trained specifically in dealing with dementia-related issues such as memory loss, confusion, and behavioral changes. They also offer structured routines and activities designed to stimulate cognitive function and slow the progression of the disease.

Moreover, these facilities have round-the-clock medical support which confirms immediate response during emergencies - something that might not be possible with home-based hospice care.

Another crucial aspect is caregiver stress. Taking care of a loved one with dementia can take a significant emotional toll on family members. Full-care facilities help reduce this burden by providing professional assistance while allowing family members to focus on spending quality time with their loved ones without the constant worry of their medical and daily living needs.

Therefore, based on this scientific evidence, if your loved one has been diagnosed with dementia, considering a full-care facility could be a useful option. It's essential to remember that every situation is unique; thus, you should discuss all available options with healthcare professionals before making any decisions.

Scientific research indicates that there are distinct differences between full care facilities and hospice care for people with dementia, and these differences significantly impact the caregiver's experience.

A study published in the Journal of American Geriatrics Society found that caregivers who opted for hospice care reported higher satisfaction levels than those who chose full care facilities. The study revealed that hospice services, which focus on providing comfort and quality of life rather than aggressive treatments, can reduce hospitalizations and improve symptom management. This results in less stress for both the patient and the caregiver.

Moreover, another research conducted by the National Institute on Aging showed that caregivers of dementia patients often experienced high levels of emotional stress and physical strain because of the demanding nature of round-the-clock caregiving. On the other hand, those who utilized hospice services reported better mental health outcomes as they received support from a team of professionals trained specifically in end-of-life care.

So if you're a caregiver faced with this difficult decision, it's important to consider not only what is best for your loved one but also what will be most manageable for you. While full-care facilities may offer more comprehensive medical treatment options, opting for hospice care could provide a more holistic approach focusing on comfort and quality of life while reducing your stress levels.

Remember: caring for yourself is just as crucial as caring for your loved one. It's okay to seek help when needed - doing so can make you a better caregiver in the long run

Chapter 16

Understanding Legal ISSUES

Chapter Overview:

- Navigating advance healthcare planning
- Setting up the right to make decisions on your behalf
- Making choices about life-saving choices

Getting diagnosed with dementia is a lot to take in. You're probably feeling all sorts of emotions and grappling with what this means for your health and day-to-day life over time. It's more than just understanding the medical side; there's a practical side to your life to think about too, like who will handle your care and manage money matters if you can't anymore. While you're coming to terms with the diagnosis, it's also super important to start planning for the future. Don't wait; while things are still clear, take the time to sort out important things like legal documents and healthcare plans.

Remember, doing all this planning early on means it's your choices that count, especially when the times comes that you might not be able to voice them anymore. It brings peace of mind to you and your loved ones knowing everything is taken care of according to your wishes.

Creating an Advance Directive (a Living Will)

Advance directives, also known as living wills, are essential documents that serve as a route for individuals to express their wishes regarding medical treatments they would prefer to decline in the future should they be unable to make such decisions or communicate them at that time. These specific preferences can cover a wide range of medical interventions and are especially critical during times when an individual may lose the capacity to articulate their choices regarding their health care.

In more formal terms, having an advance directive means that your healthcare preferences will be honored when you are no longer capable of making decisions for yourself - legally referred to as "lacking capacity." The criteria for determining whether someone has the capacity to make such critical decisions are outlined in the Mental Capacity Act 2005.

Understanding the Mental Capacity Act 2005

The Mental Capacity Act of 2005 is a legislative framework instituted to protect individuals who might not have the ability to decide on important life matters, including medical and financial decisions. This act is not only applicable in the healthcare setting but extends to various scenarios involving substantial decisions.

The primary intent of this act, as described by the United States's Ministry of Justice, is to promote autonomy. It ensures that individuals who are unable to make certain decisions for themselves still retain maximum control over their lives. In essence, it advocates for the person's rights to participate in decisions affecting them as much as possible. If unable to make decisions, any actions taken must reflect their best interests.

Outlined at the official Ministry of Justice website, the act is built upon five fundamental principles:

1. The presumption of capacity - every adult is assumed to have the capacity to make their own decisions unless it is proven they cannot.

2. Support to make a decision - individuals should be provided with all the necessary assistance before they are considered unable to decide.
3. The right to make unwise decisions - making a choice that others do not agree with does not necessarily mean an individual lacks capacity.
4. Best interest - any decision made on behalf of someone without the capacity should be for their benefit.
5. Least restrictive option - interventions or actions taken should limit the person's basic rights and freedoms as minimally as possible.

These guiding principles are designed to cater to people facing various medical challenges, such as those with severe mental health issues, neurological conditions, or cognitive impairments like dementia.

Defining 'Capacity' within the law

According to the law, individuals who lack capacity are those who cannot perform one or more of the following:

- Understand information relevant to a decision.

- Remember (retain) information long enough to make a decision.
- Weigh the given information to reach a decision.
- Communicate their decision by any means.

Importantly, the assessment of a person's capacity is decision-specific, which means it focuses solely on a person's ability to make a decision about a particular matter at a specific time. This approach recognizes that someone's mental capacity may fluctuate; a person with dementia might struggle with complex financial decisions yet can express clear preferences about simple healthcare options.

The Procedure for Assessing Capacity

Making an assessment of someone's capacity is typically the role of healthcare professionals like General Practitioners (GPs) or specialists, who often consult family members and primary caregivers during the evaluation. This assessment process involves clear communication about the decision in question to provide the individual the best opportunity to understand, remember, and deliberate the information, and finally to express their decision.

The healthcare provider seeks to establish whether the individual can comprehend the intricacies of the information provided, retain that information sufficiently to deliberate a choice, weigh the various aspects of the decision based on the information, and then convey a choice effectively.

Determining 'Best Interests'

When someone is found to lack the necessary capacity, the Mental Capacity Act stipulates that any action taken or decision made on their behalf must prioritize their "best interests." This concept goes beyond mere medical benefits and encompasses the person's emotions, beliefs, and values.

Decision-makers, often primary caregivers, physicians, or social workers, are entrusted with this responsibility and must adhere to specific guidelines to ensure that the person's rights and preferences are respected. A "best interests" decision involves careful consideration of the person's past and present wishes, feelings, beliefs, and values that would influence their decision if they had the capacity, along with consultation with family members and anyone else who might be involved in their welfare.

Creating an advance directive is a profound act of self-determination. It requires thoughtful reflection on your values and wishes concerning your medical care, and it ensures peace of mind knowing that these wishes will be respected even when you might not be able to express them. It is advisable to regularly review and update your living will as your circumstances or preferences change, ensuring that it always represents your current wishes.

When someone can't make decisions for themselves, it's crucial that we still involve them as much as possible. It's important to really understand what they would want and how they feel. This means talking to other people who are helping to look after them and making no judgments based on their age, what they look like, their health, or how they act. And remember, just because someone can't decide now doesn't mean they won't be able to in the future, so we should always consider whether they might get that ability back.

Understanding Advance Directives – Your Voice, Your Choices

An advance directive is like your game plan for future health care decisions. Think of it as you taking the driver's seat for choices about your health, in case a day comes when you're not able to speak for yourself. It's all about what care you would want (or not want) if you need someone else to call the shots.

Here's what you can decide with an advance directive:

- Whether you'd want to be revived with CPR (cardiopulmonary resuscitation)
- If you'd be okay with receiving intensive care treatments
- Your thoughts on getting blood transfusions
- Using antibiotics and IV fluids to treat you

Your choices in an advance directive have real power. Doctors need to follow what you've written down because it's all legally recognized. Essentially, it's like you're there in the room, making those decisions in real time.

But there are a few things you can't use an advance directive for:

- You can't request specific treatments that you do want here.
- It won't apply if you're dealing with severe mental health situations.
- You can't ask for anything illegal, like help in ending your life.
- It's not a place to refuse basic, comforting care (like keeping you clean and comfy).
- You can't say no to food and water with this.

What's great is as long as you're able to express yourself, your current wishes will always come first, even if they're different from what's in your written directive. Advance directives give you peace of mind, knowing your healthcare choices will be respected, always.

Crafting Your Advance Directive:

Preparing an advance directive can be a significant step in taking control of your medical care. Recognizing the importance of such documents, especially for individuals facing conditions like dementia or terminal illnesses, numerous organizations offer aid. The Alzheimer's Society, along with institutions like Macmillan that support terminally ill patients, have made example forms for advance directives available on their websites for downloading. These facilitate the process, ensuring that you can express your medical preferences clearly.

However, acquiring an official form isn't an absolute necessity. What is crucial is including all essential details to make your advance directive legally sound and easily interpreted by healthcare professionals. If you decide to create one for yourself, be sure to include:

Essential Information in Your Advance Directive

- **Personal Details:**
- Your full name
- Your date of birth
- Your current residential address
- **Medical Contact Information:**
- Your General Practitioner (GP)'s full name
- The GP's contact details, including their address and phone number
- An indication of whether your GP possesses a copy of your advance directive
- **Validity Declaration:**

- A clear statement affirming that the advance directive should be consulted and followed in the event you're unable to make decisions on your own
- **Medical Directives:**
- Detailed instructions about what medical treatments you refuse
- Precise circumstances under which your refusal should apply
- **Document Authentication:**
- The date of document completion
- Your signature to validate the directive
- Signatures from at least one witness, along with the date

For directives that involve refusing life-sustaining treatments, you must significantly assert your decision with a declaration like, "I refuse this treatment even if my life is at risk as a result."

Engage With Healthcare Professionals

It's advised that you discuss potential medical scenarios with your GP before finalizing and signing your directive. This conversation is crucial as it helps you comprehend the future impact of refusing certain treatments – understanding the possible symptoms, how they can be managed without specific treatments, and the potential consequences on your life expectancy.

Examples of how you might articulate your medical wishes after such an in-depth discussion include statements like:

- "Should I be diagnosed with a terminal illness like cancer and lose consciousness, leaving me unable to eat or drink without assistance, I refuse artificial feeding and hydration even if my life is at risk."

- "In the event that I develop a condition where death is imminent, possibly within days or weeks, I wish only for treatments that alleviate discomfort without artificially prolonging my life, even if foregoing certain treatments may place my life at risk."

Periodic Review Important

Due to the changing nature of medical conditions and personal perspectives, it's also highly recommended that you review your advance directive regularly with your family, caregivers, and healthcare providers. Remember, this document is not set in stone – it can be updated, amended, or completely withdrawn at any point should your circumstances or views evolve.

Putting together an advance directive requires careful thought and attention to detail. By including all the necessary information and involving your healthcare provider in the process, you're ensuring that your medical care respects your wishes even if a time comes when you can't articulate them yourself. Regular reviews and discussions with your loved ones and caregivers will keep this living document in alignment with your current preferences and health status.

Figuring out who needs to see your advance directive might come as a sigh of relief. Good news—you don't have to hire a lawyer to draw one up, which is definitely easier on your wallet. Once you've got your advance directive done and dusted, make sure to share it with the folks who take care of you. This way, they'll have it on hand just in case.

Here's a heads-up on who you might want to loop in:

- Your family doctor (GP)

- Any specialists you're seeing
- That awesome nurse who knows your case inside out
- Your social worker, if you have one
- The person closest to you (like your next of kin)

And hey, if you've got a lawyer, hand them a copy too—it's always good to have all your bases covered.

Exploring Lasting Power of Attorney

If you or someone you care about has dementia and might not be able to make decisions down the road, setting up a Lasting Power of Attorney (LPA) could be a smart move. It's essentially a plan where you pick a person, or people, you trust to make big decisions for you if you're not able to. An LPA is a legal paper where you (the person making the LPA) name someone to be your 'attorney'—not the lawyer type, but someone who acts for you. This person will have the authority to make calls on your behalf if there comes a time when you can't.

There are two kinds of LPAs to think about:

- One is for health and personal welfare.
- The other is for property and financial matters.

You can set up either one or both, depending on what you need. It's about giving you peace of mind, knowing that if you're unable to take part in making a decision, there's someone you trust who can step in for you.

Health and Welfare Lasting Power of Attorney

A Health and Welfare Lasting Power of Attorney is a legal paper you fill out to pick someone who can decide things for you if you can't. Things like:

- What you eat and wear every day
- Your medical care, including what treatments you're okay with or want to skip (like saying no to surgeries)
- If you should move into a different living situation, like a retirement home
- Decisions about life-saving measures

This person, your attorney, only steps in if you're not able to make choices yourself. But if you have specific wishes written in an advance directive (like a living will), your attorney has to stick to those unless you've said in the directive they can decide differently.

Property and Financial Affairs Lasting Power of Attorney

Another kind of paper, the Property and Financial Affairs Lasting Power of Attorney, lets you choose who can handle your money stuff. These people, also called attorneys, will be able to:

- Pay your bills
- Get your benefits
- Sell your house if needed

Unlike the Health and Welfare type, this one can be used as soon as it's ready, as long as you say it's okay, even if you're still able to make your own decisions.

Why Having a Lasting Power of Attorney Matters

The idea is simple: be ready for whatever comes. If you set this up while you can, you're making sure you're taken care of just the way you want. You pick the right people to look after you.

Having all this sorted out early is good because then everyone who helps take care of you knows what you want down the road. This is super important if you're alone or if your family doesn't always agree on things. It keeps peace and makes sure no one makes choices for you that you wouldn't like. Doing this now also saves trouble and money later. If you haven't set it up and you can't make decisions, going through court to settle your matters is expensive and hard on everyone. And the last big point – by choosing who your attorneys are, you avoid any chance of a stranger or someone you don't trust being in charge of your life.

Establishing a lasting power of attorney involves nuanced procedures that can vary based on your location. When selecting an attorney, the chosen individual(s) must be over 18 and could be a family member, a friend, a professional (such as a lawyer), or your spouse or partner. Trust and reliability should be the primary criteria for this choice, prioritizing individuals who are not only close to you but also responsible and financially stable. It's essential to avoid appointing someone who, despite being enjoyable company, might not be in a good position to manage financial affairs, like someone who is deeply in debt or legally bankrupt, as the latter are explicitly prohibited from serving as an attorney.

The application process for a lasting power of attorney requires completing a designated form obtainable from the

Office of the Public Guardian, part of the Ministry of Justice. This form can be accessed and filled out online, downloaded for postal submission, or requested for those who prefer analog methods. Part of the application includes nominating a certificate provider, a role that can be filled by someone who has known you for at least two years or possesses the professional qualifications necessary to attest to your understanding of the implications of granting lasting power of attorney. This is typically a general practitioner or solicitor.

Following the completion of the form, it must be registered with the Office of the Public Guardian, a process that can be initiated by either the individual granting power (the donor) or the designated attorneys themselves. Before registration, up to five personal acquaintances are to be informed about the application, allowing them a three-week period to express any objections.

The registration process, which includes certifying a copy of the lasting power of attorney, marks the final step. Should you be capable, you may certify this yourself; otherwise, a solicitor or, in certain cases, a stock exchange member, may complete it. The overall process, from initiation to completion, spans approximately eight weeks and incurs a cost, though discounts may be available based on financial circumstances.

The procedure initiates with drafting the document with a solicitor's assistance, followed by certification of capacity and submission of a registration form to the Office of the Public Guardian of your country. At times, the process involves the creation of an enduring power of attorney document by a solicitor, which is then registered with the High Court's Office of Care and Protection.

The Court of Protection plays a crucial role in cases where individuals cannot make decisions due to incapacity. The court can appoint deputies, make decisions regarding medical treatments, and handle disagreements related to lasting power of attorney, among other responsibilities. Engaging with the Court of Protection entails paperwork, hearings, and associated fees, with decision-making processes extending up to 16 weeks.

Thus, initiating the process of setting up a lasting power of attorney promptly is advisable to ensure your affairs are managed according to your wishes without undue delay or complications.

Talking About Your Choices for Emergency Medical Care

Deciding how you wish to be treated in a medical emergency is a crucial part of planning for the future, especially concerning the delicate subject of resuscitation. An advance directive is a legal document where you can record your preferences about medical treatments, including whether or not you would want to be resuscitated should you experience a significant medical event such as cardiac or respiratory arrest.

It's vital to think about and understand this crucial issue because in the event of a severe medical emergency, time is of the essence. Imagine a scenario where you are unable to communicate, and paramedics are called to your location. In such cases, these emergency medical professionals are obligated to perform life-saving measures, including CPR (cardiopulmonary resuscitation).

Paramedics are trained to respond quickly and take every possible action to save a person's life, which includes performing resuscitation procedures like chest compressions which can be quite forceful, and using defibrillators to deliver powerful electric shocks to your heart. They will also use needles to administer medications or establish intravenous lines as part of standard resuscitation efforts. However, having a Do Not Resuscitate (DNR) order available can inform the emergency responders of your wishes to not undergo such extensive measures, particularly if you desire a more peaceful passing without aggressive medical intervention. A DNR is a request to withhold CPR or advanced cardiac life support in case of a cardiac arrest. This order ensures that natural death occurs without any delays due to medical interventions that you have opted out of in your advance directive.

Without a DNR, paramedics will do their utmost, following their protocol, to bring you back to life. They will act with the best intentions, following their duty to provide care, unless there is clear instruction provided by you indicating otherwise. It's important to have these discussions and documentation ready and easily accessible, for it's in those critical moments that such paperwork will make all the difference. Informing your family, caregivers, or anyone who might be present during an emergency about where this document is located can be just as important as filling out the DNR itself.

In the event of your death, if you are content with the thought that your life should not be artificially extended by medical technology, it's essential to ensure that your healthcare preferences are documented and respected. This is not just about making a choice for yourself, but also about providing guidance and easing the burden on loved ones who would otherwise have to make these tough decisions on your behalf. Advanced planning allows you to control how you want the final moments of your life to be managed and ensures peace of mind for you and your family.

When you're managing your healthcare, there's a particular form you need based on your local area. This form gathers pretty important info about you, like:

- Your full name, where you live, your birthday
- Details about your doctor – their name, where their office is, and how to contact them

In this document, there's also a part that explains why doctors believe that performing CPR (that's when someone tries to restart your heart or breathing when it stops) may not be right for you. Usually, there are some reasons the doctor has to consider, and they need to check off at least one, such as:

- CPR probably won't get the patient's heart or lungs working again.
- There's no real benefit to the patient if their heart or lungs were restarted.
- The downsides of treatment could outweigh the positives, meaning it's not the best choice for the patient.
- The patient has clearly stated they don't want this kind of resuscitation attempt.

The doctor then confirms either that you're able to make this decision and you've talked about it with them and your closest relative, or if that's not the case, that they've had the same talk with the person legally designated to make decisions for you.

A date's also set to check the form again because situations can change, and it may be possible to cancel the DNAR (Do Not Attempt Resuscitation) order in the future.

It's crucial to understand that 'do not resuscitate' doesn't mean 'do not care for'. If medical staff see this form, they'll still do everything they can to handle your symptoms well, keeping you as comfortable as possible. They won't take you for emergency care or start CPR if your heart or breathing gives out, but they're still going to take great care of you in every other way needed.

Informing the Necessary People About Your DNAR Form

If your family doctor has talked to you about your "Do Not Attempt Resuscitation" (DNAR) form, they'll make sure to tell anyone who should know about it. However, if this conversation happened at a hospital or with a different doctor, you'll want to give your GP a copy too, so they're in the loop.

Your GP will inform all healthcare professionals who might be involved in your care, especially during emergencies, that you have a DNAR. This group includes:

- The local ambulance crew
- Any hospital specialists you see
- Doctors who provide after-hours care

It's also crucial to talk with your friends and family about your DNAR form and your wishes. In an emergency, they might instinctively call 911 because they want to help. Without your form or an understanding of your wishes, you might receive unwanted treatments or end up spending a long night in the emergency room.

The Case of the "Do Not Resuscitate" Tattoo

In a unique turn of events, an 81-year-old lady from Norfolk, England, got a tattoo in 2011. She wanted to leave no doubt about her resuscitation preferences if she were unable to breathe or her heart stopped. She had "DO NOT RESUSCITATE" inked boldly across her chest. To cover all bases — just in case she was found face-down — she had "PTO" (please turn over) on her back.

Even though she had an advance directive in place for 30 years, she explained to the media that her tattoo was her way of making absolutely sure there was no confusion about her wishes. Still, as medical ethics experts mentioned to the press, her unique approach wouldn't have a legal stand. Paramedics would have to perform CPR if they didn't see the official directive. It's essential to have clear, lawful directives established, and to communicate them with relevant parties to ensure your wishes are followed.

Guardianship

We know that dementia, a neurodegenerative disorder, can significantly impair an individual's ability to make sound decisions about their health and financial matters. As the disease progresses, individuals with dementia may lose their capacity to understand the implications of their choices, leading to situations where they might be exploited or put themselves at risk.

In such cases, guardianship becomes a critical tool for ensuring the safety and well-being of patients with dementia. A guardian is a legally appointed person who has the authority to make decisions on behalf of someone who is unable to do so themselves because of mental incapacity.

Guardianship is a court-ordered role where an individual (the guardian) is appointed to make decisions on behalf of another person (the ward) who cannot make decisions for themselves because of mental or physical disability. A guardian has more comprehensive control over the ward's life compared with an agent under a POA, including making personal and healthcare decisions.

According to a study published in The Journal of Aging Studies, guardianship can provide numerous benefits for individuals with dementia. These include improved medical care management, protection from financial exploitation, and better quality of life. However, it's important to note that guardianship should be **considered as a last resort** when all other less restrictive choices have been explored and found not enough.

A study published in the Journal of Aging & Social Policy emphasizes the importance of family members or close friends stepping up to become legal guardians for those diagnosed with dementia. This is due to the progressive nature of the disease, which gradually impairs cognitive functions, including decision-making abilities.

Guardianships are not without challenges - obtaining guardianship can be a complex process involving court proceedings and assessments by medical professionals. Therefore, it's essential to seek professional advice from an attorney specializing in elder law as soon as possible after diagnosis.

Additionally, support groups and resources like Alzheimer's Association provide valuable information on navigating through these challenges.

According to experts in elder law, there are several steps involved in getting guardianship for a dementia patient:

1. Consultation with medical professionals: It's crucial to ask with doctors who can assess the patient's mental state and provide evidence of incapacity.

2. Petitioning for Guardianship: A petition must be filed in court stating why the person needs a guardian.

3. Court Evaluation: An evaluator will meet with the person in question and send a report back to court.

4. Hearing: A judge will review all information presented and decide if guardianship is necessary.

It's important to note that becoming a guardian is not an easy task - it involves taking on significant responsibilities including making financial, healthcare, and lifestyle decisions for someone else.

So while this process may seem daunting, remember that your actions are driven by ensuring your loved one's best interests are met – which ultimately brings peace of mind knowing they're protected legally as well as physically and emotionally.

Healthcare proxy

Science suggests that becoming a healthcare proxy for a dementia patient can be emotionally challenging, but it is often legally necessary and can provide significant benefits to the patient.

According to a study published in the Journal of American Geriatrics Society, dementia patients who had designated healthcare proxies received care more aligned with their personal values and preferences than those without. This shows that having someone legally authorized to make decisions on behalf of the patient can lead to better quality of life outcomes.

When all your decisions are made with empathy and respect for the person's autonomy (even if it's difficult because you may not agree with their choices), you provide them with dignity and peace during an incredibly challenging time.

However, this role also comes with legal responsibilities. As a healthcare proxy, you are expected to make decisions based on what you believe the person would have wanted or what is in their best interest if their wishes are unknown. This requires understanding the patient's values and beliefs before they become incapacitated.

So, there's definitely immense responsibility in being a healthcare decision-maker for someone with dementia.

It is important though, to seek legal advice when considering becoming a healthcare proxy as laws vary by location. It might also be useful to join support groups or forums where others share their experiences navigating this complex process.

Chapter 17

Ten Tips for Caring for Someone with Dementia

Chapter Overview

- Keeping a sense of normalcy
- When to seek professional caregiving help
- Remembering to take care of yourself

When you're close to someone who has dementia, you often become their caregiver by default. It's a role that can just fall into your lap, whether you feel ready for it or not.

Caring for someone with dementia is tough, even when there's a lot of love there. Dementia can really change how a person thinks and acts, which means the care they need is pretty special. And the truth is, you might not see yourself as caregiver material. Maybe you figure you're too swamped with your own life, lack the patience, or just can't handle the mess that sometimes comes with the job. Yet, here you are, stepped into the caregiver shoes, and it isn't exactly a stroll in the park. Here are ten simple tips to help anyone new to caring for a person with dementia. These hints aim to make things smoother and, hopefully, bring some fulfillment along this challenging journey.

1. Keep Living Life to the Fullest

When someone first learns they have dementia, they can usually keep up with their daily activities. At this early stage, they may still work, drive, enjoy hobbies, and hang out with friends. If that's possible, we should support them in doing so. A bit more help might be needed due to dementia's early symptoms, but generally, life can continue as before for quite some time. It's not a rapid decline – it's more like life moving at its own pace.

Staying active and involved also helps to boost their morale after the tough news of a dementia diagnosis. Encouraging them to make their own decisions and maintaining their usual routine as much as possible is key.

2. Think Ahead with Compassion

While we don't want to paint a grim picture of the future for the person we're caring for, it's wise to address financial and legal matters early on while they can actively participate. Taking care of these essentials can bring peace of mind to both of you:

- **Handling Finances**: Meeting with a financial advisor to review income, expenses, and savings will help in planning for retirement and any future care needs. This way, they'll have a clear picture of their financial situation.
- **Preparing a Will**: People usually have preferences regarding who should inherit from them and who should handle their estate. Tackling this early removes a significant burden.
- **Setting Up Direct Debits**: Memory troubles can make bill-paying difficult. Setting up automatic payments for regular bills means there's no chance of forgetting them, which is one less thing to worry about.
- **Exploring Benefits**: There are many benefits available for individuals with dementia and their caregivers. Applying for these benefits early ensures that you won't miss out on any financial support. The Citizens Advice website can help you figure out which benefits to claim.

- **Arranging Power of Attorney**: Eventually, someone with dementia will need a trusted person to manage their affairs. You can set up two types of power of attorney: one for personal welfare and another for financial matters. This doesn't necessarily require a lawyer; you can download the forms from the government's website.

Offering practical advice and taking proactive steps can make living with dementia a bit easier. It's about balancing the here-and-now with practical planning for the future, all done with care and understanding.

3. Keep Their Health in Check

Caring for someone with dementia means helping them stay healthy just like anyone else would. It's likely you'll need to gently remind your loved one about their daily health habits. Start by making sure they eat well, aiming for a balanced diet with those important five servings of fruits and veggies each day, not forgetting to drink plenty of water. Encourage them to avoid too much fat and alcohol, reminding them to keep these things moderate. Smoking is a no-go. Real talk – it might take some persistence to reduce any drinking and smoking habits, and you'll need to be realistic about their food and drink preferences as dementia progresses. Just do what you can.

Next up, exercise is a biggie. It's good for everyone's heart, can lift moods, provides a chance to get out and meet others, and doing enough can lead to a good night's sleep. Exercise really is a winner all around.

And don't forget the basics like hygiene. You might have to nudge your loved one to wash their hands after they've used the bathroom and before they handle food, to put on clean clothes if theirs are dirty and to brush their teeth before bed.

4. Regular Health Check-Ups are Key

Keeping health problems at bay before they start. Make good use of this, especially when you're caring for someone with dementia. These days, it's not often you get something for nothing.

Speak to their doctor and plan out regular health check-ups, sticking with the same one if you can to keep things consistent. If you notice any changes in dementia symptoms, book an appointment pronto. Nurses can be fantastic for this too, say for regular blood pressure checks.

Don't forget to loop in other health pros - dentists, opticians, foot doctors, and pharmacists all play their part. Make sure all those important shots and screening tests, like smear tests and breast exams, are up to date.

5. Behaviour Changes – There Might Be More Behind Them

The road of dementia comes with its share of twists and turns. When you see a change in behavior, it's not always just the dementia getting worse. Everything from a simple infection to pain they can't quite tell you about could explain why things are different.

If someone with dementia suddenly pulls back, stops eating, or resists bathing, they could be scared, unsettled, or hurting. If a once easy-going person starts showing aggressive behavior, that's also a sign that something might be up. When there's a shift for no clear reason, it's best to check with the doctor or a dementia nurse to see if there's some other health issue needing attention.

6. Accepting Professional Help

When it comes to caring for a loved one, it's natural to feel that you should be the one to provide all the support they need. However, this mindset can leave you feeling overwhelmed and exhausted. It's important to remember that accepting professional help is not something to feel guilty about. Professional carers dedicate their lives to helping others and are trained to provide top-tier care and support. Imagine this scenario: by allowing experts to handle some of the more routine tasks, such as housekeeping and meal preparation, you'll have more energy and time to spend with your loved one, engaging in activities you both enjoy. This quality time can be much more rewarding than the time spent on chores.

It's worth considering the various support services available, such as home care assistants who can come into your loved one's home and provide personal care, meals on wheels services which can deliver hot meals daily, or making modifications to your loved one's home by the local authority to make it more accessible and safe, thus reducing the stress and time you would spend on these tasks. These services are designed to ease your load while also ensuring your loved one receives the best possible care.

7. Continuing Involvement After Moving to a Care Home

When your loved one transitions to living in a care home, your role in their life doesn't end; it simply changes. You become an indispensable bridge between their past and their new environment. Introduce your family member to the care home staff, share stories and details about her life so they can get to know her quickly and provide personalized care.

By bringing personal items from home to their new space, you help maintain a sense of familiarity and comfort. Regular visits are crucial, not only to monitor their care but also to continue participating in their life. Join in on the social activities the care home organizes, as these can be enjoyable for both of you. Don't underestimate the joy that children can bring to those in a care home. Encourage visits from younger family members whenever possible. Creating photo boards or displays about their life can be a wonderful way for staff to understand more about the person they're caring for, which can lead to more compassionate and personalized attention.

8.   Planning for End-of-Life Care

Although it might be difficult to think about, end-of-life care is a critical part of caring for someone. Ensuring that your loved one's wishes are understood and respected can bring great comfort to them and to the family. If they're still able to make decisions, have open discussions about their preferences and document them. When your loved one is no longer capable of expressing their wishes, it's important to gather family members and maybe include care home staff to talk about the person's potential end-of-life care preferences. Consider discussing where they would prefer to spend their last days—whether at home, in the care home, or in a hospital.

The use of advance directives, previously known as living wills, is a way to formalize these decisions. Your general practitioner (GP) can guide you through creating an advance directive, ensuring that everyone involved understands and can follow your loved one's end-of-life wishes.

9. Self-Care for Caregivers

Maintaining your own health and wellbeing is just as important as caring for your loved one. It's vitally important to look after your own physical and mental needs. Eating a balanced diet, getting enough sleep, exercising regularly, and managing stress are all crucial for caregivers.

Make sure to keep up with your own health appointments, especially if you have ongoing medical conditions like diabetes or hypertension. Staying healthy fuels your ability to provide care and support. It's also essential to have emotional and psychological support outlets, like close friends to talk to or support groups to join. Organizations such as the Alzheimer's Society offer networks for support and can provide resources tailored to the unique challenges of caring for someone with dementia. Remember, if the stress of caregiving becomes too great, don't hesitate to speak with your doctor. They can help identify additional support options or refer you to counseling or therapy if that's what you need.

10. Taking Breaks from Caregiving

Never underestimate the importance of taking time off from your caregiving responsibilities. Whether it's an evening out with friends, a weekend getaway, or even a short vacation, these breaks are vital for maintaining your wellbeing. When there's no one within the family who can step in, look into professional respite care services. These can range from day-sitters who can watch over your loved one for a few hours to arranging short-term stays in a care facility, allowing full-time caregivers like yourself a much-needed pause.

Enjoying a break isn't something to feel remorseful about—it's a necessary part of ensuring you can continue to provide the best care for your loved one without compromising your own health and happiness.

Conclusion

This book has been a comprehensive guide that traverses the complex and multifaceted landscape of dementia, from its initial symptoms to advanced stages, and from conventional treatments to supportive care. It stands as a beacon of hope and understanding in a realm often shrouded in confusion and despair. By demystifying the diseases that lead to dementia and offering a compassionate lens through which to view them, this book aims to empower readers with knowledge, support, and practical advice. It encourages an empathetic approach towards those afflicted, emphasizing the importance of maintaining dignity and respect for all individuals navigating this difficult path.

The journey through these pages is not just about understanding dementia as a medical condition but also about recognizing the human stories behind the diagnosis. It's about acknowledging the challenges and the profound impact dementia has on families and communities worldwide. The book underscores the urgent need for continued research, enhanced care strategies, and a collective effort to support those affected. As we look towards the future, it is clear that dementia is not merely a challenge for the medical community but for society at large. The strategies, insights, and stories shared within this book aim to fortify caregivers, enlighten readers, and spur action among stakeholders to address the growing issue of dementia with compassion, innovation, and resilience. Through increased awareness and understanding, we can all contribute to creating a world where dementia and its impacts are met with the strength of knowledge and the power of community, ensuring a better quality of life for those affected and their loved ones. This book, dedicated to all those touched by dementia, is more than a collection of information; it is a call to arms in the fight against the disease, a source of comfort for caregivers, and a tribute to the enduring human spirit in the face of adversity. May it serve as a guide, a source of solace, and a beacon of hope for the road ahead.

Thank you!

Thank you for choosing this book to read. It would mean so much to me if you would leave a review on Amazon. Your time is greatly appreciated!

Made in the USA
Monee, IL
26 February 2025

13022406R00122